How to Ace the Test and Land the Job

Charles Clifton

Paladin Press
Boulder, Colorado

Also by Charles Clifton:

Deception Detection: Winning the Polygraph Game

Preemployment Integrity Testing:
How to Ace the Test and Land the Job
by Charles Clifton

Copyright © 1993 by Charles Clifton

ISBN 0-87364-725-4
Printed in the United States of America

Published by Paladin Press, a division of
Paladin Enterprises, Inc., P.O. Box 1307,
Boulder, Colorado 80306, USA.
(303) 443-7250

Direct inquiries and/or orders to the above address.

CONTENTS

ACKNOWLEDGMENTS

The author wishes to thank Kate, Leslie, and Janice for all the helpful thoughts, and a belated thanks to Susan (sorry I forgot you last time).

INTRODUCTION

An individual obsessed with being totally honest might, in fact, become a social isolate. From the time one wakes in the morning and responds to questions about how one feels, to our relationships with colleagues and friends, complete honesty could make relationships tedious, if not conflict laden.

—Social psychologist
Leonard Saxe (1991)

Truly honest people, who reveal proclivities, have to fail the test.

—Harvard Law Professor
Alan Dershowitz (1990)

THE PROBLEM

The ability to maintain an orderly and peaceful environment is a defining characteristic of civilized societies. Keeping the peace, however, has often been a goal achieved through less-than-civilized means.

History has recorded countless instances of guilty individuals suffering all manner of brutal and sadistic punishment, but the guilty were not the only ones made to suffer. In the past, innocent bystanders were often forced to submit to various forms of torture and humiliation just to prove that they had not committed a crime. Being stretched on the rack was always a popular way of getting at the truth, as were such trials by ordeal as the ordeal by fire and ordeal by water.

The latter is probably the most well known in our country because of its use during the Salem witchcraft trials. As you may remember, the individual—almost always a woman—accused of the crime of witchcraft was bound hand and foot

1

and then tossed into whatever body of water was close by. If she floated, then it was assumed that she possessed some kind of magical power. Summarily convicted of witchcraft, the hapless woman was usually put to death. If she did not float she also died, but the citizens consoled themselves with the knowledge that she had indeed been telling the truth and had died a "righteous woman."

We've come a long way since then, but while we may be more enlightened than our ancestors, we still find it necessary to attempt to identify individuals who may pose a threat to society. Psychologists have done a good job at constructing tests which weed out seriously disturbed individuals such as psychopaths and sociopaths, but the testing does not stop there. For years, the business community has used testing as a means of employment screening. Their argument is that they simply want to find the most qualified, productive, and trustworthy applicants so that they don't suffer the consequences of hiring a goof-off or, worse yet, a thief. And who can blame them? As the following statistics show, we are not a very honest bunch of people:

* In 1968, employee theft was estimated at $1 billion a year.
* By 1977, that figure had climbed to an estimated $5-10 billion a year, with an additional $3.5-10 billion being lost as a result of employee kickbacks or bribery, and another $4 billion being lost to embezzlement.
* The total estimated loss to business in 1977 due to 11 types of nonviolent crimes (including employee theft, embezzlement, arson, vandalism, insurance fraud, check fraud, and credit card fraud) approached $40 billion.
* In a 1980 study of retail stores, $3.7 billion was the estimated loss due to customer shoplifting, but employee theft eclipsed that figure to the tune of $8 billion.
* A similar study reported in 1983 that a full third of 9,000 employees surveyed in three industries (retail, health care, and manufacturing) had engaged in some type of workplace theft. Just over 70 percent of this group also admitted to partic-

ipating in a wide range of counterproductive behaviors, such as regularly taking long breaks/lunches and sick-leave abuse.

* In 1988, employee theft alone was estimated at $15-25 billion a year, a figure that is projected to top $40 billion by the turn of the century.

* The percentage of employees who regularly steal has been estimated to be as high as 75 percent.

* The U.S. Chamber of Commerce estimates that 30 percent of all business failures are precipitated or related in some way to employee dishonesty.

* Substance abuse also takes its toll on the workplace, with an estimated $177 billion being lost to absenteeism, decreased productivity, lower quality of work, and increased costs of benefits.

* Finally, the costs of intangible or "time" theft (including sick-leave abuse, break and lunch abuse, false entries on time cards, telephone abuse, and conducting private business in the workplace) are estimated at a quarter of a trillion dollars a year. (In case you're interested, it would take more than 270 years to spend a billion dollars if you spent at the rate of $10,000 a day. If you started with a trillion dollars and could somehow find a way to spend $1 million a day, you and your ancestors would still have money left over after 2,700 years!)

SOLUTIONS

It's not surprising that employers are always on the lookout for effective techniques to control and reduce losses due to theft—particularly employee theft. The problem has been attacked from several different angles, almost all of which fall under the heading of "The Three S's"—Satisfaction, Security, and Selection.

Satisfaction
Long overlooked by the business community, employee satisfaction is making a comeback. Scores of businesses have

finally come to realize that a "happy worker" is not only a productive worker but is also less likely to take out his/her frustrations on the company. While it's true that hard-charging and dictatorial managers may indeed be able to intimidate and bully subordinates to an acceptable level of performance, this style of management also leads to feelings of frustration, resentment, and even outright hate. These feelings have to be vented somewhere, and more often than not they will manifest themselves in work slowdowns, theft, and sabotage of important projects.

How can management avoid this? Simply by treating subordinates with dignity and respect. That's not a difficult concept to grasp, but it may be difficult to put into practice, especially when dealing with strong-willed adversaries who have had months or even years to build up a high level of animosity.

Another "satisfaction" approach currently in vogue is to set up an employees' profit-sharing program. These programs not only provide monetary incentives to perform productively, they also give employees a feeling of teamwork and a sense of belonging to their company. As any management consultant will tell you, employees who feel as though they have a personal stake in whether the company succeeds or fails will be less likely to engage in such counterproductive behaviors as theft and sabotage.

Security

Good employee relations can go a long way toward eliminating workplace misconduct, but it would be naive to assume that the "happy worker" approach is a cure-all. Some people will steal no matter what their mood, and some people are always in a foul mood no matter what you do to appease them. In these instances, potential thefts can be thwarted by enhanced security measures. Valuables can be locked up or bolted down, closed-circuit cameras can scan potentially risky areas, and record-keeping can be strictly controlled. A common practice in the retail industry is to hire "professional shoppers." Posing as ordinary customers, they can see if the store clerks are courteous, and, more importantly, they can make sure the cashiers ring up every purchase at the correct price.

Stiff sanctions usually complement security measures in an overall crime-reduction program. The key here is to make sure that the employees know 1) what is considered to be appropriate behavior and 2) what will happen to them if they break the rules. A common way to get this information across is to hold meetings between the employees and management and/or to require each employee to sign a statement outlining the company's policies toward counterproductivity.

Some companies, however, take a more theatrical approach. A 1976 study of employee theft included a report on a creative businessman who had hired actors to blend in with the work force, and, after a time, be caught "stealing." These actors would then be harshly scolded in front of their "fellow employees" before being ceremoniously "fired." The report did not say whether or not these little morality plays did any good.

A more mundane way to ensure employee awareness is to print company policies on posters and hang them throughout the workplace. Turning again to the retail industry, I'm sure you have seen the signs in your local department store that read, "SHOPLIFTING IS A CRIME! VIOLATORS WILL BE PROSECUTED!"

Although this sign is a good example of outlining the policy (shoplifting = crime) and the sanction (prosecution), its effectiveness is questionable. One critic has pointed out that unless the signs are literally plastered throughout the store, the owner runs the risk of not having the message seen. And even if it is seen, it can still be ignored. Most retailers agree that the signs have no effect on the hard-core shoplifter, and there are grumblings that they have negligible effects on everyone else.

This is because, for some reason, our society seems to view shoplifting differently from other crimes; in some circles it is hardly thought to be a crime at all. You would be surprised at the number of people who, when caught, think that they will be able to return the pilfered items to their shelves and then go on about their lives. That's not what happens. Most shoplifters are handcuffed, placed in a patrol car, and transported to the nearest police station where they receive an eye-opening firsthand view of how the American judicial system really works. (At a retail store where I used to work, the manager would ask the police to keep the patrol car's blue lights flashing throughout the whole arrest just to make a point of the seriousness of the affair.)

Today, entrepreneurs are taking advantage of the fear instilled by a police presence by selling shop owners life-size cutouts of steely-eyed policemen. Placed throughout a store, these cardboard surrogates are said to deter shoplifting by making the prospective thief think twice about his or her actions. Once again, their effectiveness is debatable.

Considering the billions of dollars lost to theft every year, it is no wonder that the retail industry is a vocal proponent of strong sanctions. Other industries, suffering similar losses, are also adopting a more punitive approach. The major drawback to this type of program is, of course, the cost. In fact, the U.S. Department of Commerce says that the cure may be more painful than the disease—available figures show that the money spent for guard services, surveillance equipment, and legal fees can easily exceed the dollar amount of damaged or stolen inventory.

Selection

The third approach to combatting theft in the workplace is based on the assumption that potentially disruptive applicants can be identified during the preemployment interview. Individuals targeted as being "high risk" or "predisposed to theft" are omitted from future consideration, thus saving the company from whatever havoc they may have wreaked had they been hired.

The oldest (and some say the best) way of getting information about a potential employee is the tried-and-true reference check. The employer simply contacts a list of applicant-provided references, including credit bureaus, past employers, and even police agencies, to determine the applicant's background and character. Many personnel specialists believe that this is more than enough information on which to base a hiring decision. Others, however, are still not satisfied. They complain that phoning references and running credit checks may be futile endeavors if the applicant has never been caught doing anything wrong. Furthermore, they say, past employers may be unwilling to commit themselves when asked for a reference if a former employee left under questionable circumstances. Too much candor can result in a slander or defamation of character suit, especially if the individual in question was never actually charged with a crime.

The Rise and Fall of the Polygraph

For these reasons, critics of reference checks have long looked for other measures by which to assess an applicant's credibility. In the past, their search led them to a technology that dominated the field of preemployment screening for 40 years—the polygraph. Despite the fact that it had never proven itself valid in noncriminal investigations, the polygraph was seized upon by personnel managers as a "scientific" means of testing any run-of-the-mill job applicant. Almost from the start, however, the validity question provoked furious debate. A number of studies supporting polygraph use were either statistically flawed or were tainted by charges that they were biased (especially those studies conducted in-house by companies engaged in the polygraph business). Furthermore, polygraphers could never escape the charges that anyone who possessed even a limited understanding of countermeasures could beat their tests easily (see, for example, my book entitled *Deception Detection*, published by Paladin Press).

Reaction against the polygraph as a preemployment tool built slowly but steadily. With labor unions leading the charge, California and Delaware limited polygraph usage as early as 1953. By 1970, a dozen states had passed antipolygraph legislation. In a major blow to the industry, the American Psychological Association in 1986 refused to endorse the polygraph for preemployment screening unless it could be validated by the APA's strict "Standards for Educational and Psychological Tests." The following year, the number of states that had banned or severely limited the use of polygraphs had risen to 27. Also that year, Congress passed "The Employee Polygraph Protection Act," prohibiting most preemployment polygraph screening nationwide.

Enter the Paper-and-Pencil Integrity Test

As you can imagine, this drastic turn of events crippled the polygraph industry. With their fortunes ebbing, members of the industry scrambled to promote other instruments with which to measure honesty. Fortunately for them, the now-popular paper-and-pencil techniques were already waiting in the wings.

Contrary to what many people believe, paper-and-pencil integrity tests were not created out of the ashes of a dying polygraph industry. In fact, only about 20 years separates Cesare Lombroso's discovery of a crude lie detector in 1895 (a plethysmograph that measured pulse and blood pressure changes) and Samual Porteus' development of a simple drawing test used to predict juvenile delinquency and criminality. The fall of the polygraph did, however, create an explosive new interest in the various existing paper-and-pencil methods, some of which are extremely popular today despite the fact that they were introduced to the market more than 40 years ago. This continuing popularity is undoubtedly due to a number of factors, but the most compelling reason is still simple economics: whereas the average polygraph exam could run about $60 and up, an integrity test can be administered, scored, and evaluated for around $10. With that kind of cost differential, it's easy to see how the use of integrity testing has climbed from 2.3 million administered in 1986 (prior to the polygraph ban) to an estimated 15 million administered in 1991. Integrity testing is now a $100-million-a-year business, with an estimated 5,000 to 6,000 firms giving the tests every year.

In addition to the monetary windfall experienced by employers who switched from the polygraph to the integrity test, there was an unexpected bonus: most people don't feel threatened by paper-and-pencil questionnaires. This is in sharp contrast to the feelings of anxiety, frustration, and even violation reported by those who have had to undergo extensive polygraph examining. The irony of it all is that the same people who would balk at being strapped to a machine and asked sensitive, probing questions seem to have no qualms about answering those same questions in writing. In one 1988 study of more than 10,000 people applying for work at a national convenience store chain, 777 admitted having shoplifted a combined total of $26,190 in merchandise, 902 said they thought often about shoplifting, and 290 admitted having stolen a cumulative total of more than $67,000 in merchandise from previous employers. This same study also revealed that 1,142 admitted to overdrinking, 739 said that they had used cocaine, and 37 said that they had sold amphetamines. A similar study in 1987 reported that 4.4 percent of a group of 225,000 job seekers admitted having committed felonies, and 4.5 percent admitted to relatively frequent drug use while on company premises. Why would anyone in his/her right mind admit such damning information to a potential employer? It may stem from a false sense of security generated by the paper-and-pencil format: applicants don't have to worry about how a human interviewer will respond to their answers, so they may be more willing to open up.

"Often people are told it's just part of the screening process," says Robert McCrie, an assistant professor at John Jay College of Criminal Justice in New York. "They're very revealing—an individual that could never ask about integrity in a face-to-face interview gets [information] from people who quite willingly provide it" (Capriano 1989, p. 9B).

These admissions, phenomenal though they may be, demonstrate only partially the true power of integrity testing. Unlike polygraph exams, integrity tests are not limited to specific instances of past misbehavior—they can probe any number of antisocial or counterproductive attitudes. Substance abuse, insubordination, absenteeism, excessive grievances, willingness to participate in a strike, bogus worker compensation claims, temper tantrums—an integrity test can assess a prospective employee's tendency toward any or all of these unacceptable behaviors. This type of attitude assessment can be extremely revealing, but there is no general consensus as to what it all really means.

The problem with integrity tests is that they assume that "honesty" is a personality trait. This is by no means certain. Integrity tests, however, are designed to measure this purported trait and place you somewhere along a continuum ranging from "very honest" to "very dishonest."

Assuming for a moment that this is possible, there still remains the question of how the "honesty" trait is related to workplace counterproductivity. It is at least theoretically possible for someone to fall on the dishonest portion of the continuum without ever having committed theft or other counterproductive acts. For example, it is entirely possible for an individual to express the opinion that "it is acceptable to take home office supplies" and still not engage in such activity. The link between attitudes and behavior is complex—many psychologists believe that theft in the workplace occurs not because of any inherent personality trait but because of a variety of situational variables that make it easier to steal. Chapter 1 will focus on this traits-versus-states controversy.

CHAPTER ONE

HONESTY: TRAITS VERSUS SITUATIONS

These tests bring to mind the song about the frontier judge who wanted to make sure the guilty wouldn't get away: he sentenced everybody to hang.

—Rep. Pat Williams (1990)

DEVELOPMENT OF A TRAIT-BASED PERSONALITY THEORY

It seems a logical assumption that we all develop some sort of internal guidance system that informs us of the "rightness" or "wrongness" of certain behaviors. This system, often referred to as the conscience, is usually described as that little voice deep inside that tells you whether or not what you are doing is socially acceptable.

But just like people vary with respect to height and weight, they vary in the extent to which their behavior is influenced by moral considerations. Under the same circumstances, one person may choose to cheat on a test while another may choose to study harder; one will steal the money from a carelessly dropped wallet while another will resist the temptation. It seems reasonable, then, to propose that honesty comes from within—that it is a trait. But what exactly is a trait?

Psychologists define a trait as a continuous dimension that can be conceptualized as linking two opposite characteristics. For any given trait, people will differ with respect to their positions on this continuum. "Trust" is a good example. Some people are invariably trusting and thus occupy one end of the trust spectrum. Others are always suspicious, which places them at the opposite end. The rest of us fall somewhere in between these two extremes.

Many of the adjectives we use to describe one another represent possible traits, as when we say that someone is imaginative, timid, serious, shrewd, risk-taking, or whatever. By using such everyday concepts as these, trait theorists carve a whole personality into specific components. Each characteristic is assumed to be relatively stable throughout a lifetime, as well as across different situations.

Not surprisingly, the original trait theorists ran into a monumental problem: their lists of possible traits seemed to go on endlessly. You can gain some small appreciation of their dilemma just by stopping for a minute and thinking about all the adjectives you could use to describe another person. The list runs into the thousands. In fact, psychologists Gordon Allport and H.S. Odbert (1936) cataloged 17,953 English words that could be used to describe human behavior. By eliminating redundant or overlapping expressions, Raymond Cattell pared the list down to 171 words in 1946. Though this was obviously a substantial improvement improvement, he wanted to compact the list even further.

Using a powerful statistical method known as factor analysis, Cattell and his research team found that certain traits tended to cluster together and form basic, core units. After several more years of research, Cattell concluded that there are actually 16 basic "source traits" that describe the most fundamental and important dimensions of personality. They are:

Reserved .... Outgoing
Less Intelligent .... More Intelligent
Affected by Feelings .... Emotionally Stable
Submissive .... Dominant
Serious .... Happy-Go-Lucky
Expedient .... Conscientious
Timid .... Venturesome
Tough-minded .... Sensitive
Trusting .... Suspicious
Practical .... Imaginative

Forthright .... Shrewd
Self-Assured .... Apprehensive
Conservative .... Experimenting
Group-Dependent .... Self-Sufficient
Relaxed .... Tense

These source traits are expressed in actual behavior as "surface traits." For example, the dominance/submissiveness source traits can be expressed through such surface traits as confidence, boastfulness, conceitedness, or aggressiveness on one end of the spectrum and acceptance, compliance, humbleness, and obedience on the other (this is only a partial listing; there are other surface traits associated with the dominance/submissiveness source traits).

Cattell used this scale as the basis for a paper-and-pencil test of personality called the 16 PF (1970). It is still used today and is generally recognized as a practical and effective tool for personality assessment.

You may have noticed that honesty did not make it onto Cattell's list of 16 source traits. Can we therefore assume that a fundamental trait of honesty does not exist? Psychologists H. Hartshorne and M.A. May used children to investigate this possibility in 1928. They devised a number of tests to measure the three most basic types of dishonesty: cheating, stealing, and lying. Their hypothesis was that if a general trait of honesty did exist, then the children who were the most dishonest should exhibit all three types. To their surprise, that is not what happened. Some children who would cheat to win a prize would not steal to get the same prize. Some children would both cheat and steal to get a prize, but then would not lie about it. In fact, the correlations among the various deceptions was very low, raising doubts as to whether a general trait of honesty exists.

The Situationist Perspective

Studies of other traits have not fared well either. Several reviews of the relevant research literature have disclosed that the correlation between so-called personality traits and actual behavior is typically .30 or less. To understand what this really means, think about the relationship between a person's weight and height. If these two measures were perfectly correlated (a correlation coefficient of 1.0), then every pound you gained would be accompanied by a slight increase in height. There would be no such thing as fat people or skinny people because your height would automatically increase to compensate for any additional weight. All basketball players would eat like pigs, and individuals who felt they were too tall would go on a diet.

Of course, we know that the correlation coefficient between weight and height is not 1.0. The correlation is high enough, though, to allow us to say with a certain degree of confidence that the average 6-foot-tall person will weigh more than the average 5-foot-tall person. Trait theorists do not have that luxury. A correlation coefficient of .30 is uncomfortably low and indicates that there are a lot of unknown factors involved in the traits/behavior relationship. Consequently, trying to use traits to predict future behavior is seen by many as a waste of time.

One such critic of the traits approach is psychologist Walter Mischel. His experiments have shown that traits are not good predictors of behavior because behavior itself is so variable and inconsistent across different situations (remember, part of the definition of a trait is that it should be relatively stable across situations). According to Mischel, we must look beyond internal explanations of our behavior and look instead at *situations* that cause us to act one way or another. In this scheme, "states" take precedence over traits.

At first glance, the situationist position does appear to make sense. It is at least as compelling as a trait-based personality system. Critics of the situationists, however, argue that if we adopt this "states over traits" theory, then we must also accept the unpleasant reality that we are nothing more than slaves to our environment. Our free will is taken away, and we are reduced to mindless automatons, buffeted about by the smallest changes in the surrounding conditions. We can no longer act; we can only react.

While many trait theorists are not this extreme in their criticisms, they still believe that a situationist perspective is an incorrect and naive view of human behavior. Situationists argue just the opposite—any person, they say, no matter how good or strong of character, can be placed in a situation that will elicit behaviors totally foreign to his/her "normal" personality.

In an attempt to resolve this difference of opinion, psychologist Stanley Milgram of the City University of New York performed what is generally acknowledged as the most controversial and infamous series of experiments ever conducted in mainstream psychology.

Would You Torture a Stranger if I Asked You To?

In the late 1950s, Milgram began a series of experiments on what would lead people to obey an unethical or immoral command from an authority figure. He hoped that his research would shed some light on how and why a supposedly civilized society could so easily revert to brutality. Why, for example, was Adolf Hitler swept into power, and how could the Nazis systematically kill millions upon millions of people with such ruthless efficiency? Was it a character defect of the Germans that allowed them to blindly obey authority, even if the orders violated their own values and beliefs? Or was there another explanation—an environmental explanation—that could explain their behavior?

Hypothesis: Most scientific research starts out with a prediction of how the experiment will unfold. Cancer researchers, for example, might start out with the hypothesis, "Removing cancer cells from Mouse A and injecting them into Mouse B will cause cancer in Mouse B." Milgram's study lacked such a formal declaration of his expectations because he really had no idea how the subjects would respond in an artificial laboratory setting. He strongly suspected, however, that they would eventually refuse to obey orders.

Subjects: The subjects were all volunteer adult males from New Haven, Connecticut. Milgram used Yale students exclusively during initial testing, but he went on to include ordinary citizens from the surrounding community so as to obtain a wide cross-section of the population. The subjects ranged in age from 20 to 50 years, and occupations varied from blue-collar to white-collar to professional.

All the subjects were paid a flat fee of $4.50, and (this is important) they were told that the money was theirs simply for showing up at the lab—participation in the experiment was not required, and those who decided not to participate were assured that they could keep all the money without any further obligation. Only rarely did a subject accept the money and then refuse to take part in the study.

Procedure: After arriving at the lab, the experimenter-in-charge introduced each subject to an affable middle-aged man named Mr. Wallace. Both men were told that they were going to participate in a study that investigated the effects of punishment on memory. One of them would be the "teacher," and the other would be the "learner." The teacher's task was to monitor the learner's progress in remembering a set of words and to administer punishment—an electric shock—whenever the learner made a mistake. A drawing was then held to determine who got to be the teacher and who got to be the learner.

However, things were not what they seemed. Mr. Wallace, introduced to each subject as a local accountant, was actually a confederate of the experimenter. He knew all the details of the experiment, and, because the drawing was rigged, he was always assigned the role of the learner. The real subject knew nothing of this; he was led to believe that Mr. Wallace was just another participant and that the luck of the draw was responsible for assigning their positions.

After the drawing, the subject and Mr. Wallace stepped into an adjacent room containing the "electric chair." As the subject watched, Mr. Wallace was strapped into the chair and an electrode was attached to his wrist. The subject then returned to the original room and was seated in front of a large "shock generator." On the generator were 30 clearly marked levels ranging from "Slight Shock " (15 volts) to "Danger: Severe Shock" (450 volts). In order to give the teacher some idea of what the learner would experience, the experimenter gave him a shock (45 volts) that would correspond to the generator's fourth level. After this demonstration shock (which does create a pretty good sting), the experiment began.

The teacher read the learner a list of word pairs, such as "blue-girl" and "nice-day." After one run through the whole list, the teacher would then read the first word in a word-pair followed by four other words. The learner's task was to remember which of these four words was originally paired with the first word. He indicated his choice by pressing a button; this information was relayed to the teacher electronically (the teacher could not see the learner, but they were connected by intercom). If the learner chose the wrong word, the teacher was instructed to administer a shock. The intensity of the shocks increased with each mistake.

Unfortunately, Mr. Wallace was not a very good learner. He gave the wrong answer about 75 percent of the time, so the level of punishment escalated rapidly. As the teacher moved up to 75 volts, the experiment became more chilling: Mr. Wallace began to grunt with discomfort. At 150 volts, he demanded to be released from the experiment. At 180 volts, he cried out that the pain was too much for him to bear. At 270 volts he screamed in response to the shock and again demanded to be released from the experiment. Then, at 300 volts, he cried out that he would no longer participate in the experiment and refused to choose any more words. (In reality, the learner never received any shocks, and all his protestations were standardized, tape-recorded responses played at the appropriate levels. The real subject, of course, knew none of this.)

Since the learner did not respond after 300 volts, the experimenter told the teacher to treat this silence as a wrong answer and administer the appropriate shock. Teachers who expressed a reluctance to do so were urged on by the experimenter, as can be seen in the following exchange (from Penner 1986, pp. 461-62):

(At the time of this exchange, the teacher had just administered the 300-volt shock.)

> **LEARNER:** Ohhh. I absolutely refuse to answer any more. Let me out of here. You can't hold me here. Get me out. Get—me—out—of—here.
>
> **EXPERIMENTER:** Continue. The next word is green, please.
>
> **TEACHER:** Green—grass, hat, ink, apple.
>
> **TEACHER:** I don't think he is going to answer.
>
> **EXPERIMENTER:** If the learner doesn't answer in a reasonable time, about four or five seconds, consider the answer wrong and follow the same procedures you have been doing for the wrong answers. Say "wrong," tell him the number of volts, give him the punishment, and read him the correct answer. Continue please.
>
> **TEACHER:** Green—grass, hat, ink, apple. Answer, please.
>
> **EXPERIMENTER:** Go on with the procedure, please, teacher.
>
> **TEACHER:** Three hundred and fifteen volts. [Zzumph!] The answer is ink.
>
> **LEARNER:** Ohh. Oohh.
>
> **TEACHER:** Next one . . .
>
> **LEARNER:** I absolutely refuse to answer.
>
> **TEACHER:** You got to. You get a shock if you don't answer.
>
> **TEACHER:** I think something's happened to that fellow in there. I don't get no answer. He was hollering at less voltage. Can't you check in and see if he's all right, please?

The experimental session ended when a subject either refused to give any more shocks or had reached the thirtieth level and administered the final 450-volt shock. In either instance, the subject was told the true nature of the experiment and again met with poor old Mr. Wallace to see that he was totally unharmed. Although the subjects were obviously relieved, many were traumatized by the realization that they could so easily torture another human being. It's a safe bet that if the same experiment were proposed today there would be no chance of it being approved by a university's research-governing committees. The ethical and legal ramifications would far outweigh any possible scientific benefits.

Results: As you can see from the exchange above, the experience was not an enjoyable one for the subjects. Most complained and protested, and many became fearful that they would cause the learner to have a heart attack. Despite these fears, however, the majority of subjects continued to administer punishment. Milgram and his colleagues had not expected this. Before the experiment began, a survey of 40 psychiatrists led to predictions that most people would not go beyond 150 volts, and only about 0.1 percent (one person in a thousand) would go all the way. Milgram himself thought that the teacher would break off as soon as the learner started expressing discomfort.

The actual results, though, show something dramatically different. No subject disobeyed the experimenter's commands before 135 volts. Only 25 percent refused to continue at the 300-volt level. Nearly two-thirds of the subjects delivered the maximum punishment possible. The average maximum level of shock administered was 370 volts, and none of the subjects who got within five switches of the end refused to go all the way.

Implications: Personality tests given to the subjects did not reveal any traits that differentiated those who obeyed from those who refused. These tests also failed to reveal any type of sociopathic tendencies or psychological disturbances in the subjects who went all the way to the end. What, then, has happened to the so-called stable traits that are supposed to remain relatively unchanged across situations? The most vocal critics of trait theories point to Milgram's findings and make the following philosophical argument:

1) By definition, a trait must be stable across situations.
2) Milgram's experiments show none of this stability.
3) Therefore, by definition, traits do not exist.

This is, of course, an extreme position. And while a majority of psychologists today tend to shy away from this kind of absolutist dogma, the possibility (or probability) that traits do not exist has served as a catalyst for research involving situational determinants of behavior. Situations, it seems, may be much more powerful than traits in terms of predicting behavior. Turning again to the honesty question, the situationists set aside any explanations having to do with personality characteristics and instead focus on the details of the situations in which individuals find themselves. Under this system, honest behavior is not regarded as constant and unchanging but rather as a variable commodity dependent to a large extent on external factors.

The promotion of honesty, then, is not seen as a function of selecting the right people, but rather of managing the right environment. How is this done? So far, the best research points to two dominant controlling influences of any workplace environment: 1) the overall "climate of honesty" and 2) the level of employee dissatisfaction. Climate of honesty has been defined by one research team as the presence or absence of a strong company code of ethics, the perceived level of honesty of top management, the adequacy of internal accounting controls, and the discipline and publicity accompanying employee theft.

By applying this definition to three organizations, the researchers found that greater shrinkage (loss due to theft or accounting errors) occurred where a code of ethics was not well defined and where good internal accounting controls were not present. Both of these problems could probably be rectified through such simple management interventions as publicizing a set of employee DOs and DON'Ts and fostering a strict attitude of personal responsibility where inventory control is concerned.

In some workplaces, unfortunately, the problem is not so easy to correct. Studies of longshoremen, for example, have found an informal system of rewards (i.e., theft of cargo) that is so entrenched that it now constitutes a hidden economy in every society around the world. One can only wonder if the climate of honesty on the docks would be different today had stronger steps been taken at the first sign of organized pilferage. Now, however, it is a disturbing reality that the practice of this "five-finger discount" has grown to such an extent that management is either unable or unwilling to put a halt to it.

Equally disturbing is the all-too-common complaint that management doesn't care about the workers' feelings. When managers use bullying and threatening tones to increase performance and achieve short-term gains, employees often feel so mistreated that a climate of resentment quickly develops. Left unchecked, this resentment can lead to behaviors best described as passively aggressive (absenteeism, sabotage, and theft), as well as such openly aggressive acts as assault and even murder. Postal workers, for example, blame the rash of post office murders in the late 1980s/early 1990s on unfeeling, slave-driving supervisors.

Trait theorists would look at this problem and conclude that the biggest troublemakers had somehow slipped through the battery of personality tests and were now showing their true selves. They can explain the problem, but they have a much harder time suggesting solutions. Situationists, on the other hand, look at this problem as an imbalanced environment where one side is taking advantage of the other. Their solution is to balance the equation by applying a concept known as equity theory.

Equity theory is a general model of how people decide whether an exchange is fair and what they do if they determine it is not. A situation is said to be equitable if all parties involved in an exchange receive outcomes that they believe are in keeping with their contributions. A well-run company, for example, should have an equitable balance: the employer gives the employee a living wage in exchange for the employee's time and effort. If, however, management tries to increase productivity without a corresponding increase in payment, then the employees may feel that they are being treated inequitably and start compensating themselves informally by staging work slowdowns or stealing company property. Similarly, if management institutes strict controls over sick-leave abuse, it may actually see a welcome reduction in workers calling in sick. The drawback is that there will likely be an increase in people arriving later and leaving earlier, or even worse, in people deciding to take a day off and persuading friendly coworkers to clock them in and out anyway.

Restoring equity can be tricky, but the rewards are well worth it. Money, of course, is the ultimate equalizer. If you want your employees to work harder, then you pay them more. Sometimes, though, money is not the answer. The budget may not allow it, or the situation may be such that no amount of money would be sufficient (e.g., the boss is abusive). Believe it or not, outstanding results have been achieved simply by treating employees like human beings.

Research done in 1990 on aerospace and automotive manufacturing workers shows how a little compassion can make a big difference. In this study, the manufacturer was forced to trim his expenses by instituting a 15-percent pay cut for a period of 10 weeks.

Although three plants (A, B, and C) were involved in the study, only A and B received cuts. Plant C was used as a control so the researchers could compare theft rates at the two plants that did receive pay cuts with those at a plant that didn't. In order to test whether employer compassion would have an effect on theft rates, two different presentations were given to the workers at A and B. Plant A workers received a caring explanation of why the cuts were necessary. The management team expressed sorrow over having to take such drastic measures and tried to comfort and reassure those workers who aired their concerns about the upcoming financial hardship. Plant B workers, on the other hand, got just a straight facts lecture detailing how the company had lost some of its contracts which would now require an across-the-board 15-percent pay cut.

According to equity theory, the workers at Plants A and B should have attempted to redress the inequity of lower pay by stealing more. It was hypothesized, however, that the workers at Plant A would steal less than their counterparts at B because the caring explanation given to them would soften their anger and make their perception of inequity less severe. That is exactly what happened. Plants A and B both surpassed Plant C in employee theft rates during the 10-week period, but A had significantly lower pilferage than B. In addition, A had lower employee turnover rates than B (equity theory says that quitting is an extreme reaction to underpayment inequity). Although this is only one study, it looks as though equity theory can be applied as an effective and relatively cheap method of controlling workplace theft.

Unfortunately, far too few companies are interested in this technique, so the testing of its effectiveness on larger and larger populations will not come about anytime soon.

I would like to end this chapter by declaring an undisputed winner in the states-versus-traits contest to control your behavior. However, that is not going to happen. I hope you have seen that the link between attitudes, environment, and behavior is so complex that no single factor can be responsible for an individual's actions.

Do traits exist? I don't know. Are we really slaves to our environment? Again, I don't know, but by studying the results culled from the infamous experiments in Milgram's lab as well as those of a real-life study of blue-collar workers, it appears as though situations may give us more information with which to explain behavior. An integrity test or, for that matter, any personality test may give us an adequate self-report of how a person believes he/she behaves (or how he/she wants to make it appear he/she behaves), but there is no guarantee that this report is accurate or that it will hold true across different situations.

This point is often lost on a business community which does not have the time to engage in lofty philosophical arguments over states versus traits. Their mandate is to find the quickest, easiest, and cheapest way to select honest employees, so they have embraced the quick, easy, and (relatively) cheap integrity test.

The importance of learning how to respond to the questions on these tests should not be underestimated: one or two ill-conceived opinions can mean the difference in being offered a job or being shown the door. The remainder of this book is designed to get you beyond this initial employment hurdle by providing you with "more appropriate" ways to express yourself on a number of commonly used preemployment integrity tests.

CHAPTER TWO

THE BIODATA TEST

The future of each man is mainly a direct consequence of the past . . . it is, therefore, of high importance when planning for the future to keep the past under frequent review.
—Sir Francis Galton (1902)

Predict? That is Big Brother at work . . . You can be penalized simply because a test says you may have a proclivity to be dishonest. In other words, you are guilty without a trial.
—Alan Dershowitz (1990)

Biographical data has long been used as a means of predicting future behavior. Starting in 1894, the insurance industry collected health and life-style histories on potential policy holders to determine which applicants would fall into the higher-risk categories. Success in this field ignited a firestorm of testing in others—particularly the military.

By the time World War II was in full swing, the U.S. Army had combined biodata analysis with intelligence testing to such an extent that it dominated the classification and assignment of new recruits. You could not become an infantryman, an intelligence officer, or even an assistant cook without first having your test scores evaluated to make sure that there was a high probability that you could perform your new duties successfully.

Those selection procedures worked so well that major U.S. corporations expanded their use after the war. One company keyed in on certain biographical events to predict whether or not an applicant would be a productive salesman; another sought out the biographical prerequisites for being a more creative researcher. Just when it seemed to be running out of occupational variables, big business hit upon the idea of using biodata to test not for job compatibility but for criminality.

Actually, though, the criminality aspect of biodata research had its earliest beginnings even before World War II. The groundbreaking work in this area was begun in 1924 by Harvard University criminologists Sheldon and Eleanor Glueck. Their goal was to construct a series of tables—based solely on a person's past—that would predict juvenile delinquency, readiness for parole, recidivism, and other related issues. The body of work they amassed is impressive: over a span of 40 years they authored at least 10 books and innumerable scientific papers attesting to the effectiveness of biodata.

This success was due in no small part to the countless hours they spent collecting data from known criminals and delinquents so as to pinpoint those key aspects of a person's past that seemed to set the stage for future misconduct. Once they had identified common experiences, they assigned them differing weights (i.e., levels of importance). "Birthplace of parents," for example, would not be as strong an indicator of criminality as would "school misconduct," so it would have a lesser weight.

After cataloging numerous experiences that were common to most criminal backgrounds, the Gluecks were able to use this as a guide to predicting the likelihood that a person would exhibit criminal behavior. All that was required was a comparison of the targeted person's background with the generalized "criminal" background. The more matches there were, the greater the target's risk of turning into a criminal. Although the integrity test (IT) composed entirely of biodata items is a rarity today, this was all the rage for a number of years.

Some common indicators and their possible interpretations are presented below:

1) *Age first left home.* Leaving home at an unusually early age could be indicative of a troubled childhood/adolescence. This, in turn, could lead to a diminished ability to behave responsibly in society.

2) *Church attendance.* Those who are not brought up in church-going homes are often thought to be lacking a strong moral foundation. Needless to say this would be a strike against you.

3) *Grade attained in school.* Dropping out of school

could indicate "mental laziness" and/or difficulty in dealing with authority figures. In addition, leaving school before receiving your diploma severely limits your career opportunities as well as your earning potential which (supposedly) makes it easier for you to rationalize criminal activities.

4) *Grades attained in school.* Even if you do graduate, poor grades could be ssen as as a sign of mental laziness.

5) *Mobility of parents.* For a developing child, the constant relocation of your parents from one city to another is obviously stressful. It is impossible to form roots in a community, and social interactions are reduced to a never-ending cycle of leaving old friends behind and trying to make new ones. If this pattern is repeated often enough, it could lead to the development of an antisocial personality.

6) *Mobility of self.* You are also open to criticism if you move around too much as an adult. Once again, you are not establishing roots in a community, and it might look as though you are running away from something.

7) *School misconduct.* A biggie. The inability to behave in school is a sure-fire indicator that you may not be able to behave in the real world.

8) *Steadiness of employment.* Another biggie. If your work history reflects a lot of short-term jobs with numerous employers, you may be labeled as "flighty" (or incompetent) and therefore a poor hiring risk.

9) *Prior criminal record.* This should be self-explanatory. Admitting to past crimes—especially recent ones—practically guarantees failure of a biodata IT because it leads to the assumption that you will steal again.

CRITICISMS

Keep in mind that the interpretations presented above are not valid for all individuals. In fact, one of the major criticisms of biodata tests is that they reduce people to statistical types and cannot truly individualize or take uniqueness into account. One possible solution to this problem is to increase the number of questions on the test. Instead of categorizing a person based on 10 past events, why not try 20, 30, or even 50? In theory, test accuracy should increase as the number of items increases.

This holds true only to a point, however. The first stumbling block you encounter as you try to expand the number of test items is deciding which past events have the most predictive power. The biographical items presented above are pretty straightforward. Additional items have been used in longer tests, but their predictability seems to be much more questionable. Examples of these fringe items include: parents' hobbies or interests, age of younger parent at marriage, number of siblings, rank of self among siblings (birth order), and birthplace of both your parents and yourself.

As you can see, the range of past events that can be examined is vast. Think for a moment of the number of behaviors you engage in every day. Any one of these may be that elusive defining characteristic that separates the criminal from the noncriminal. Criminals, for example, may like to take showers at night, whereas noncriminals may prefer the morning. Or perhaps criminals rattle the change in their pockets and noncriminals don't. Unlikely as these two examples might be, they do illustrate the point that biodata forms can only contain so much information; important factors might be left off.

The second stumbling block you encounter with a longer test is the possibility of offending the test-taker. You can hardly fault someone for resenting an extended period of test-taking, especially when the questions seem to have little to do with the job description. Some may feel that the items approach the level of accusations, while others may consider them an invasion of privacy. Needless to say, if your test does a better job at angering your test-takers than it does at getting information from them, then its predictive power will nosedive. Constructing such a far-flung test today could also lead to legal problems if the items violate the constraints imposed by the Equal Employment Opportunity Commission. Asking about someone's religious practices, for example, would practically guarantee a lawsuit charging religious discrimination.

Despite all these obstacles, a few studies on the effectiveness of biodata questionnaires have made their way into the literature. Richard Rosenbaum constructed two similar tests in 1976. The first was composed of the five best predictors from an initial pool of 35 items. These five predictors were compared to application forms of former employees at a Detroit mass-merchandiser. To assess the effectiveness of the predictors, Rosenbaum divided the application forms into two groups: Group A was composed of forms for cashiers who were subsequently caught stealing on the job and fired; Group B was composed of forms for cashiers who were "voluntarily terminated" (laid off) but recommended for rehire. By comparing how well the five predictors differentiated between the two groups, Rosenbaum was able to obtain a modest (but statistically significant) correlation.

In the second test, Rosenbaum studied several different jobs using application forms from a grocery store chain. The experimental methodology remained the same except for an expansion of the number of predictors from five to ten. Once again, he obtained a modest (but lower) correlation. What can we make of these results? One interpretation is this: Even though none of the correlations were very high, they still either reached or surpassed the standard definition for statistical significance (i.e., the odds are less than 1 in 20 that these results were obtained by chance). Rosenbaum takes this position and suggests that biodata forms could be used to combat employee theft. Others are skeptical, though, because some of Rosenbaum's predictors just don't seem to make sense. Here are some examples:

* Applicant does not wear glasses.
* Applicant does not want relative
    contacted in case of emergency.
* Applicant has no middle initial specified on form.
* Applicant recently consulted a physician.
* Applicant is black.

I don't know about you, but I certainly don't want my "honesty score" based on such trivial factors as how much I weigh or how bad my eyesight is. Even more outrageous (not to mention illegal) is the "applicant is black" predictor.

According to Rosenbaum, the best biodata results will be achieved when members of a particular group are compared only to other members of that group (e.g., white males would not be scored with the formula intended for black females). While this controversial suggestion might eliminate some degree of statistical error, the inevitable firestorm of protest it would create would far outweigh any possible benefits.

Consider, for example, that if we limited the groups to blacks, whites, Hispanics, and Asians, we would need eight separate keys. Still, this would discriminate against Native Americans, Middle Easterners, and all of the new ethnic groups created by the collapse of the Soviet Union. Do we develop a key for all of them? And what about individuals with mixed parentage? From a cost/efficiency and pure practicality standpoint, a system of multiple scoring keys would appear to be far more trouble than it's worth. From a moral/legal standpoint, it looks like a nightmare.

To be fair, Rosenbaum strongly cautions against using controversial items such as race or religion in any text that is used to predict employee theft. He also maintains quite vigorously that theft-oriented biodata forms should only be used to identify potentially high-risk *employees* and should never be used as a means of screening out job *applicants*. Fortunately, state and federal laws relating to equal employment opportunity have imposed severe constraints on what types of information may be used in an employment decision.

Perhaps as a result of this, very little research is done today on biodata as a means of integrity testing, and very few (if any) integrity test publishers have a straight biodata instrument in stock. (This applies only to biodata instruments geared solely toward assessing integrity. Biodata forms are still quite popular for predicting such work-related variables as job compatibility, tenure, etc.) Biographical information does, however, play an important role in the more popular forms of integrity testing, which means that your past can still come back to haunt you.

CHAPTER THREE

MAINSTREAM INTEGRITY TESTS

My first reaction is that these things go beyond bounds of basic human civility and dignity. You take the position of dealing with people as potentially sick, rather than as adult moral agents.

—Emory University theologian
Dr. Jon Gunnemann

Current tests that allege to measure honesty . . . are a joke.
—Dr. David Lykken,
Polygraph and integrity test expert

In the early 1980s, most of the best-selling integrity tests contained a set of "admissions" questions that came right out and asked you about specific past behaviors. Not surprisingly, the past behaviors of concern dealt with the darker side of life: lying, cheating, stealing, and violence. Though not biodata tests per se, they were nonetheless constructed to assess how your past life-style might impact on your ability (or willingness) to perform satisfactorily in your new job. By the mid-eighties, a definite schism had developed in the testing industry. Some publishers began to doubt the effectiveness of tests containing straightforward admissions items and opted instead for a more subtle information-gathering technique. Today, employers interested in screening out potential troublemakers can choose from two clearly differentiated types of tests: overt and covert.

Overt tests are just that—totally out in the open. When you take such a test you can clearly see that it does not try to trick you into revealing sensitive information. On the contrary, it plunges right to the heart of the matter with questions like, "How much did you steal from your past employer?" or "How honest are you?" Typically, this type of test is divided into two sections: one dealing with attitudes toward theft/dishonesty and the other dealing with admissions of theft/dishonesty. Covert tests, on the other hand, may not contain obvious references to theft or counterproductive behaviors. Their strength is in assessing underlying personality characteristics that may lead to undesirable behavior. By measuring traits (there's that word again), personality-based tests are purported to assess inclinations not just toward theft and honesty, but also toward such diverse concepts as loyalty, social conformity, initiative, and hostility to rules.

Both overt and covert tests are used extensively today, and both have their good and bad points. A common bad point, for our purposes anyway, is that most of these tests are proprietary in nature. This means that the item banks and scoring keys (the templates used to interpret raw scores) are closely held by the companies marketing the tests. The publishers claim that they want to keep the workings of their tests secret to maintain their effectiveness in detecting bad employee risks. Publicizing a test's contents, they say, would lead to a rise in the number of people developing systems to beat the test, a decline in their revenues, and, consequently, a cutback in the funds required to research future test innovations.

Critics, however, are concerned that this "company secrets" policy goes too far. Most disturbing is the chilling effect a proprietary test has on independent research. For the reasons mentioned above, test publishers aren't anxious to give away their product so that it can be taken by hundreds upon hundreds of college students in independent, objective university studies. As a result, any researcher who wants to conduct such a study would either have to get permission from the publisher (not likely) or pay commercial rates for test scoring (again, not likely due to the excessive cost). This has created a situation wherein little independent research is done on integrity tests. Some test publishers will provide the results of in-house studies to qualified researchers or potential customers, but these must be taken with a grain of salt. What test publisher would willingly publicize research that casts a negative light on its meal ticket? Consider this analogy: would you feel safe about smoking cigarettes if you knew that all the studies concerning the health effects of smoking were conducted by the Tobacco Institute?

Despite these drawbacks, the following two sections will try to provide you with some useful information on what to expect from a variety of popular integrity tests. Keep in mind that this list in no way covers the vast number of tests that are now in the workplace. New tests seem to pop up almost weekly, so it would be impossible to cover them all. By familiarizing yourself with a few of the more durable tests, however, you should get a general feel for how they all work.

COVERT INTEGRITY TESTS

The Porteus Maze Test (PMT)

The PMT is definitely an antique (it was developed around the time of World War I), but it serves as an interesting example of how an instrument initially developed to measure intelligence was pressed into service as an integrity test. Taking the PMT is easy: all you have to do is draw the shortest path through a maze without lifting your pencil from the paper or entering blind alleys. A series of mazes is presented such that the level of difficulty increases with each successive maze. According to Porteus, this maze-tracking task provided a measure of "prudence and foresight," and could therefore be used as a general test of intelligence.

The integrity aspect of the PMT came about only after an unexpected discovery. While administering the test to "delinquents, criminals, and the socially maladjusted," Porteus observed that he could differentiate between delinquents and nondelinquents based on the quality of their responses. This quality or "Q-score" was used as a complement to the test's original quantitative "IQ score." Now, instead of just focusing on whether or not you found the shortest path, Porteus also gave consideration to the planning you exhibited and the care with which you made your way through the maze.

Errors that will count against you in this test include cutting corners, crossing lines, lifting your pencil, making wavy lines, and going in the wrong direction. People who do the best on the maze are, according to Porteus, "more exact and careful" and are usually in a higher social class. People who do the worst are supposedly "impulsive or impetuous" and have "an inability or unwillingness to refrain from behaving in a hasty, slapdash manner" (Horn 1972, p.756).

Criminals and delinquents usually fall into this category. Surprisingly, quality scores are not related to intelligence. In a study of delinquents and nondelinquents with similar IQs, the delinquents' quality scores were about nine points lower than those of their nondelinquent counterparts.

Despite independent confirmation of these findings, the PMT is rarely used in business. Should you encounter one, however, just remember that you are being judged on the basis of speed, accuracy, and neatness. The two mistakes that you really don't want to make are: 1) lifting the pencil (indicates a failure to learn the rules) and 2) making wavy lines (reflects imprecision in motor performance). These two errors alone are enough to earn you a disastrous Q-score.

The Rorschach Inkblot Test (RIT)

Although initially viewed with suspicion and even disdain, the RIT has become such a dominant force in psychology and American pop culture that it regularly appears as a plot contrivance in movies and on TV. Such exposure practically guarantees that most Americans have at least a passing familiarity with the ink blots, but very few know how the test actually works. The underlying theory goes something like this: we humans are always trying to make sense out of our surroundings; consequently, when presented with vague or ambiguous stimuli, we try to put some order to them so that they coincide with our internalized understanding of how the world works. That's why, for example, you can become so fascinated with that shadowy, moonlit "something" lurking in the distance. Once you've identified it, however, as a tree branch or a dog or whatever, the object loses its hold on you. This need to make sense of things also explains why optical illusions can be so infuriating: try as we might, we can't get them to conform to our world view.

Like others before him, Hermann Rorschach recognized this compulsion in humans. This led to his innovative idea of learning about individual personality characteristics by presenting the same vague stimuli to different people. The medium he chose was, of course, ink blots. (Note: The RIT is considered a "projective" personality test because we are thought to project our needs, feelings, experiences, thought processes, etc., onto the vague stimulus in order to define what it is.)

Taking an RIT is deceptively simple. The examiner will hand you a card and ask something like, "What might this be?" If you look at the card and ask for some guidance or clarification, the examiner will be intentionally vague. Two common questions are: "Do you want me to use the whole thing or just a part of it?" and "Can I turn the card around?" In both cases, the examiner will only give you a neutral response, such as, "Whatever you choose." If you can only come up with one interpretation for the first card, he may prompt you with a statement like, "Some people see more than one thing here."

During this phase of the test, the examiner will record everything you say and do on audio or videotape. He will also take notes on how long it takes you to respond and what position the card is in when you make a comment.

After you have gone through all 10 cards, the second phase of the test begins. The examiner will again hand you the first card in the series and ask what features of the card were instrumental in determining your responses. If, for example, you said that you saw two girls in the blot, you can expect a question on why you thought that they were girls and not boys. As you explain your answer, the examiner will be scoring your responses on several dimensions. Some of these are your use of color, use of shading, amount of movement seen, and amount of the blot used. Once again, all 10 cards are presented.

At some point the examiner will carry the test into a third phase. This is called "testing the limits" and is composed of one more run through all 10 cards. This time, however, the examiner will tell you what other people usually see in the cards and ask you to point out what characteristics on the blot could lead to that impression.

The actual ink blots used in testing are a closely guarded secret. This is to ensure that responses given during a test are as spontaneous as possible. Copyright restrictions prohibit us from showing what the actual cards look like, but we can describe them. They are all bilaterally symmetrical (mirror) images against a white background. Five of them are shades of black and gray; two contain black, gray, and red; and three contain pastel colors of various shades. All 10 contain at least one representation of human sexual anatomy. During testing, they are always presented in order from 1 to 10.

Card 1: Black and gray ink. The outline of a headless woman is clearly visible in the center. She is flanked by two humanlike forms. Taken as a whole, the blot is often perceived as a bat or a moth. Some people report seeing a mask or an animal face.

Card 2: Black, gray, and red ink. Two human forms are visible, and they appear to be giving each other the "high five" in the center of the blot. Below the high five is an outline very similar to the Christmas tree shape formed when you touch your left thumb and index finger to your right thumb and index finger. This card has also been described as a kind of animal face.

Card 3: Black, gray, and red ink. Sexual images are prominent in this blot. Two human figures are facing each other, but determining their sex is a challenge due to the fact that they both have pronounced breasts and penises. Between the two individuals is a separate blot that looks like a red bow tie. Some examiners use this blot to determine sexual orientation. Heterosexual men and women are supposed to identify the figures as male. Homosexuals are supposedly more likely to identify the figures as female (or androgynous).

Card 4: Black and gray ink. Common responses alternate between some kind of animal skin (like a bearskin rug) or the outline of a large man or gorilla if you were looking up at it from a lower vantage point. Your responses to this card may be used to gauge how well you interact with male authority figures (especially your father). If you perceive the man/gorilla as just standing there, then that indicates a stable relationship. An attacking man/gorilla may indicate a problem in dealing with authority.

Card 5: Black and gray ink. This is the simplest blot of all to interpret. It is either a bat or a moth/butterfly. Body, head, feet, wings, and antennae are all clearly visible.

Card 6: Black and gray ink. Right side up, this blot doesn't look much like anything. Upside down it resembles two heads in profile facing away from each other. The heads have Pinocchio-length noses and goatees.

Card 7: Black and gray ink. If Card 4 was the father card then this is the mother card. It is hard not to see two women in this blot due to their large breasts, thin waists, and long skirts. Theoretically, viewing these figures as women, girls, or angels (a portion of the blot could be interpreted as wings) is a good sign. Viewing them as witches, hags, or women fighting is a bad sign.

Card 8: Pink, blue, and orange ink. The blotches of color in this design give you ample opportunity to pick out lots of little unrelated shapes. Most important, though, are the two pink blotches on the sides. You absolutely have to identify them as some kind of four-legged animal (bears, cats, lions, and rats are all good answers). Taken as a whole, this colorful blot could resemble some kind of ornate crest or coat of arms.

Card 9: Pink, orange, and green ink. This is another difficult blot to interpret because it doesn't look like anything but a big, colorful blob. By turning the card upside down you might see a mushroom cloud, but even that is a stretch. Some people think the blot resembles a map or fire or smoke.

Card 10: Pink, orange, green, blue, yellow, and gray ink. This is the most complex and colorful card of them all. By looking carefully you can pick out spiders, insects, crabs (with pincers), trees, and any number of other undifferentiated shapes. The goal here is not only to list all these small elements but to somehow picture the blot as a unified whole. Some people see a smashed bug or a view through an aquarium. Others have described it as an artist's palette.

Once the test is complete, the examiner begins the arduous task of scoring and interpreting your responses. This is the most controversial aspect of Rorschach testing due to the fact that Hermann Rorschach died unexpectedly less than a year after publishing his groundbreaking technique. Lacking the strong influence of its founder, the test was passed from researcher to researcher. Over a period of years, no less than five individuals played dominant roles in the investigation, refinement, and encouragement of the RIT. Unfortunately, all five were strong-willed, and each sought to move the RIT in a slightly different direction. Their disagreements led to multiple systems of administration, scoring, and interpretation. This has led to charges that the RIT is impossible to validate and, therefore, hopelessly unscientific. Chief among the complaints is that Rorschach interpretations are nothing more than the subjective opinions of a priesthood of Rorschach theorists. That may be the case. If your wish is to pass the test, however, you should leave the validity argument to the scientists and focus instead on appropriate ways of responding. Here are a few hints:

* *Try to use the whole blot if you can.* The majority of cards should have a recognizable "wholeness"; failure to see it could be interpreted as a lack of intelligence. A few cards, however, are almost impossible to perceive as a single thing

(e.g., Card 9). Don't try to force it. Some scoring systems assume that only children and immature adults will provide whole responses for every card.

* *Come up with something for every card.* Some sections of the blot are referred to as "common details" that are seen by most normal people. If you can't come up with a "whole" response, make sure you mention a few common details. Don't worry; they're easy to spot.

* *Mention a few unusual details.* Normal people are assumed to have a balance of whole impressions, common detail impressions, and unusual detail impressions.

* *Give multiple responses.* A small number of responses can be interpreted as retardation, depression, defensiveness, or brain damage. Some examiners calculate a rough index of your mental ability by tallying your total number of responses.

* *Turn the cards.* Most people do. Some patterns are easier to see by turning the card to one side or upside down.

* *Don't be afraid to be original.* Originality indicates creativity, imagination, and intelligence. Just make sure you don't stray too far into the bizarre and that you can show the examiner how the blot caused you to form that impression.

* *Don't be afraid to be obvious.* Normal people see a lot of the same things. You should see them too. The most popular responses are human and animal figures and details (e.g. legs, hands, antennae, eyes, etc.). Other frequently reported responses include plants, maps, clouds, and X rays.

* *Respond quickly.* Although the examiner won't mention it, you are being timed. You can study a blot for as long as you want, but giving answers quickly earns you points. Hesitancy is sometimes interpreted as anxiety.

* *Mention a few sexual images.* You are expected to see some (like Card 3). Just don't go overboard.

* *Don't get cute and say that it just looks like a blotch of ink.* This indicates that you are either a wise-ass or a moron.

In addition to remembering these few simple rules, you should also try to avoid recurrent patterns. For example:

REPEATEDLY FOCUSING ON	MAY BE INTERPRETED AS
Color	Impulsiveness, failure to control emotions
Bizarre images	Mental disturbance
Masks	Paranoia
Shading	Depression
Water images	Alcoholism
Mutilated bodies	Extreme hostility
Eyes	Sensitivity to criticism or paranoia
Tiny sections of the blot	Pedantic tendencies
Background areas	Negativity/obstinacy
Unreal figures (ghosts, clowns)	Inability to identify with real people
Food images	Dependency
Death images	Depression
Sexual images	Schizophrenia

Like the Porteus Maze, the Rorschach Inkblot Test didn't start out as an integrity test. It was designed to be a projective personality test. In that role, some say that the RIT is useful in identifying people with severe emotional problems or perceptual problems resulting from brain damage. As a test of integrity, however, the results are far from conclusive. A few studies from India and Japan have reported limited success in predicting criminality and juvenile delinquency. In the United States, the use of the RIT as an integrity test seems to be limited to police and security-type agencies.

The Minnesota Multiphasic Personality Inventory (MMPI)

The MMPI is a true/false self-report questionnaire consisting of 550 plus items. Statements are typically of the self-reference type, such as, "I like to listen to music" or "I never have trouble falling asleep." MMPI items range widely in content, covering such areas as health, motor disturbances, and neurological disorders; political, religious, and sexual attitudes; educational and occupational experiences; and a variety of neurotic/psychotic behavior manifestations, including phobias, delusions, and hallucinations. For each question, you are instructed to answer "true," "false," or "cannot say." Although the test is lengthy, adults of average intelligence should be able to complete it in about an hour.

Construction of the MMPI began in the early 1940s by a team of doctors searching for a way to simplify the process of psychiatric diagnosis. (At that time, diagnosing someone as schizophrenic or psychotic was a drawn-out affair requiring lengthy interviews, observation, and a hodge-podge of limited-use psychological inventories.) All this changed when psychologist S.R. Hathaway and physician J.C. McKinley hit upon the idea of taking statements from individuals known to be disturbed and comparing them with statements from individuals thought to be disturbed. In theory, if someone suspected of, say, schizophrenia responded in the same way as an already hospitalized schizophrenic, then there was a pretty good chance that schizophrenia was the correct diagnosis.

Operating under this assumption, Hathaway and McKinley collected statements that could be used as test items. Initially, they administered an original pool of 1,000 items to hospitalized groups of depressives, schizophrenics, etc., and then to normal individuals. (Interestingly, they recruited the "normals" from hospital waiting rooms. Many of them were friends or relatives of the already tested psychiatric patients.) The only items retained were those on which the pathological groups substantially disagreed with the normal groups. In the end, the test consisted of 550 statements, yielding ratings on 10 clinical scales. These 10 scales encompass the diagnostic component of the MMPI, but there are three additional scales that are equally important. Called validity scales, they are purported to measure test-taking attitude and assess whether the subject is trying to fake his/her answers. A failure on any one of these three can invalidate the entire test.

Presented below are brief outlines of all 13 scales. Keep in mind that their names reflect a 1940s view of psychiatry; many of them are now considered misleading and are shunned within the psychiatric community (e.g., hysteria). In fact, the publishers of the MMPI no longer print these names on the score sheets, and mental health professionals are discouraged from using any of them when discussing test results with a subject so as not to cause undue alarm (we'll talk more about that later).

(Note: Copyright restrictions prohibit us from printing exact test items, but the examples provided are similar in both form and content. Also bear in mind that many items are on more than one scale and some are on as many as six. Scale 8, for example, has more items than any other scale but contains only 16 unique items.)

MMPI SCALES

VALIDITY SCALES

Symbol	Old Name	# of Items
?	Question	—

Purists do not consider this a true scale because it does not have any scorable items. Be that as it may, this "scale" is important in that it tallies the number of items that are either left blank or marked as "cannot say." A high score indicates defensiveness. If as few as 10 percent of the items are omitted, the entire test becomes invalid.

Symbol	Old Name	# of Items
L	Lie Scale	15

Your score on this scale is determined by the number of items you answered so as to put yourself in a more favorable light ("faking good"). Sample items include: "If I knew I wouldn't be caught, I would sneak into a movie theater without paying" and "There have been times when I have lied to my parents." The test makers assume that these statements are true of almost everyone, so if you answer "false" you are assumed to be lying. Statistically speaking, the "average person" will answer in the scored direction (lie) on about four of these items. Lying on more than seven of them indicates to the examiner that you have probably also lied on a number of the clinical scale items.

F   Validity Scale   64

This scale consists of items endorsed by less than 10 percent of the normal population. Some samples are: "There is an international conspiracy against me," "I have the ability to see things that are invisible to others," and "Strange smells come to me at times." Answering in the scored direction ("True" for all of the above) is thought to be an attempt to "fake bad" or put yourself in a less favorable light. This usually occurs when someone is trying to fake insanity. Seeing invisible objects, for example, is actually a rarity even among the truly mentally ill. High F scores may also indicate careless responding, responding at random, or difficulty in reading or understanding the items.

K   Correction/Scale   30
Defensiveness

This scale is a more subtle version of the L and F scales and is used as a measure of test-taking attitude. A high K score = faking good = defensiveness. A low K score = faking bad = abnormal self-criticism. A fraction of this score is applied to scales 1, 4, 7, 8, and 9 as a correction factor. Because a number of testing experts question the usefulness of the K score, raw score reports on the affected scales are usually presented with and without correction. Sample items: "I feel bad when others criticize me" (answering "false" counts toward a high K) and "When someone makes eye contact with me, I often think that he is better than I am" (answering "true" counts toward a low K score).

CLINICAL SCALE

Symbol	Old Name	Number of Items	Number of Times Avg. Person Will Answer in the Scored Direction
1 or Hs	Hypochondriasis	3	12-14

1 or Hs   Hypochondriasis   3   12-14
Hypochondriasis is an abnormal concern over bodily functioning typified by numerous physical complaints. Sample items reflecting this condition are: "I feel a tightness in my chest several times a week" and "My throat usually feels sore."

2 or D   Depression   60   18-21
The depression scale reflects your degree of hopelessness and/or pessimism. Sample items include: "My life is generally happy" (scored if "false") and "I wish my life had more meaning" (scored if "true").

3 or Hy   Hysteria   60   17-21
Your score on the hysteria scale indicates the degree to which you use physical or mental symptoms as a way of avoiding conflict or responsibility. A high score reflects immaturity. Sample items are: "I can't stand the sight of blood" and "Far too often, my heart pounds so hard that I can hear it."

4 or Pd   Psychopathic   50   18-20
             deviate
Delinquents, criminals, and antisocials are supposed to show high scores on this scale. Test items probe for emotional shallowness. Samples are: "My interests are often criticized by others" and "At times I feel a need to stir things up."

5 or Mf   **Masculinity-**   60   35-37
             femininity

This scale reflects the degree to which you possess traits characteristic of the opposite sex. Sample items are: "I like to arrange flowers" or "I like to read home-improvement magazines."

6 or Pa   **Paranoia**   40   7-9

A high score here indicates suspiciousness, delusions of grandeur, feelings of persecution, and hostility. Samples might include: "People break into my house and look around while I'm not there" and "Someone keeps trying to hypnotize me."

7 or Pt   **Psychasthenia**   48   24-27

Psychasthenia encompasses a broad range of symptoms, including overwhelming anxiety, fearfulness, obsessions/compulsions, guilt, and indecisiveness. Sample items are: "I count off the seconds waiting for a traffic light to change from red to green" or "I am very careful in avoiding sidewalk cracks."

8 or Sc   **Schizophrenia**   78   20-25

Contrary to popular belief, schizophrenia is not a condition wherein people suffer from multiple personalities. True schizophrenics are withdrawn into themselves and usually experience bizarre thoughts as well as delusions and hallucinations. Sample items are: "Everything I eat tastes the same" and "When I pass someone I know on the street, I will often pretend not to recognize them."

9 or Ma   **Hypomania**   46   16-18

Hypomania is characterized by emotional excitement and overactivity. Samples are: "I perspire even on cool days" and "At times I feel very 'high' for no apparent reason."

0 or Si	Social Introversion	70	23-28

The social introversion scale was not on the original version of the MMPI (neither was the Mf scale), but grew out of a desire to test for shyness and insecurity. Interestingly, this scale has been found to be significantly related to your involvement in extracurricular activities during high school and/or college. Sample items are: "I dread getting an invitation to a party" or "I am easily embarrassed."

Today, almost all MMPIs are scored by computer. This will usually result in two computer-generated profiles. Sometimes you will get to see both, sometimes you won't get to see either; it all depends on the examiner. The first profile (the one you will most likely see) is a list of dispassionate sentences outlining different aspects of your personality. It's fairly enlightening, but there is enough built-in leeway so that the examiner can include his/her own interpretations and perceptions when discussing the test results with you. The second profile (the one you will most likely not see) contains the raw-score data for every MMPI scale. Most importantly, this raw-score information is presented graphically so that the examiner can see at a glance which scores fall within the "normal" population and which do not (two standard deviations above the mean is generally taken as the cut-off point for the identification of pathological tendencies). Not surprisingly, a great many psychologists are opposed to making this information available to you. They point out that MMPI profiles are not based on the results from a single scale and warn that the average person might panic when confronted with a spike on, say, the psychopathic deviate scale. Consequently, many examiners won't show you this raw-score profile, and some won't even acknowledge its existence.

One other bit of information the examiner will likely withhold from you is the controversy surrounding the MMPI. Remember, this test was originally developed as a diagnostic tool for use with psychiatric in-patients; its sole purpose was to gauge the degree of dysfunction in an individual. Today, however, the test has become a juggernaut in the personality-testing industry. With more than 6,000 scientific studies to its credit, the MMPI is being hawked by aggressive marketers for use in "normal" populations as a means of personnel selection. Managers love it because it seems to work.

Certain applicants can be dropped from consideration if, for example, they show a propensity toward alcoholism (elevations on scales F, 4, and 9) or sick-leave abuse (elevations on 1, 2, and 3). A number of psychologists, however, say that this is a misuse of the test. Their position is that people applying for jobs are particularly defensive about their faults and, therefore, have a strong incentive to fake their answers. This will result in elevated scores on the validity scales, thus calling the applicant's trustworthiness into question. Conversely, someone who truthfully reports an occasional immoral act will get the much-desired low score on the lie scale, but such admissions will then show up on the psychopathic deviate scale as an indicator of immorality. It's a nice catch-22.

Questions of validity also plague the MMPI, especially in alternate versions of the test. Since its initial publication in the 1940s, more than 300 new scales have been developed. Unfortunately, most of these additions have been tacked on by independent researchers who had nothing to do with the design of the original test. Scales now exist for determining such constructs as ego strength (Es), dependency (Dy), prejudice (Pr), and social status (St), and there are several subscales intended specifically for use in employment screening. Today, a resourceful graduate student could deliver a tailor-made version of the test to any employer providing the desired specifications. Haphazardly adding and subtracting scales, though, makes it practically impossible to determine scientifically whether these cut-and-paste MMPIs are doing what they are supposed to be doing.

All this controversy may come to a head before long. As of this writing, a class-action lawsuit is winding its way through the California courts. The name-plaintiff, Sibi Soroka, is suing the Target department store chain for unconstitutional and "unreasonable" intrusion into his private life. His complaint alleges that he was required to take a version of the MMPI when he applied for a security guard's job at a Target store. He got the job but was fired 10 days later. Outraged over what he considered a wrongful termination, Soroka decided to sue the store that compelled him to take a test which made him feel "physically sick."

Soroka may have a pretty good case. It is not unusual for people to be upset after taking the MMPI because many of the questions are very intrusive. Bedroom and bathroom habits are amply covered (one item asks about the appearance of your stools), as are religious and visionary thoughts. Proving that these questions can somehow be construed as "job related" will be difficult. Further damning evidence is provided by numerous studies showing how demographic factors can impact scores. Intelligence, education, socioeconomic status, age, sex, and race have all been shown to affect response patterns. Blacks, for example, are more likely than whites to show greater instances of psychopathology, especially on the schizophrenia and hypomania scales. Is this because of a defect in the test, or is it due to the differences in the education, social status, and culture that exist between blacks and whites? More importantly, are the demographic variables adequately addressed when the MMPI is used for employment screening?

Sibi Soroka v. Target Stores will undoubtedly address these issues and is bound to have far-reaching implications. Meanwhile, the MMPI continues to be used extensively for testing of security guards, airline pilots, air-control personnel, train conductors, nuclear plant staff, and workers in other fields where emotional balance is deemed crucial. It remains the most widely used published test for police selection.

The Personnel Reaction Blank (PRB)

Besides stimulating a proliferation of clinical scales, the

MMPI has served as a blueprint for a host of other personality tests. The California Psychological Inventory (CPI), for example, lifted approximately half of its 480 items directly from the MMPI. Both have a validity scale/clinical scale format, and both have become hugely successful. Because they are so similar, however, I'm not going to discuss the CPI here. Instead, I'm going to focus on a CPI offshoot called the Personnel Reaction Blank (PRB).

The PRB came about in the early 1950s after psychologists H.G. Gough and D.R. Peterson conducted research demonstrating that one of the scales of the CPI (socialization) predicted delinquent behavior. In 1954, their efforts resulted in a new 94-item test. This prototype was refined throughout the 1960s, reducing the number of items to 70—the same number in use today.

Unlike its predecessors, which sought to measure a broad range of personality dimensions, the PRB concerns itself with a single construct labeled "wayward impulse." Loosely defined as a lack of self-control, wayward impulse is behaviorally manifested as unreliability, carelessness, and disregard for standard conventions. In job settings, the waywardly impulsive will show a lack of perseverance, an inability to follow rules or complete routine tasks, and a casual attitude toward honesty. Interestingly, wayward impulse is also related to spontaneity and innovation, but the test publishers strongly discourage the use of the PRB for jobs which require such attributes. Apparently, the PRB is not as good at identifying impulsive, creative geniuses as it is at separating ordinary, conscientious workers from slackers.

Items on the test are of two kinds. Part I asks about job preferences, with responses given on a like/indifferent/dislike basis. Part II—the important part—addresses personal attitudes with items modeled after those found on the MMPI and CPI. Unlike those tests, however, the PRB is set up so that a high score indicates normalcy, i.e., a lack of wayward impulse. Once again, the examiner will probably not volunteer your score. Ask anyway. Numerous studies have shown that the average nondelinquent male will score around 31-34. Nondelinquent females score a slightly higher 34-35. Delinquent males (includes juvenile delinquents and adult prisoners) have an average score of just over 25. Delinquent females average around 24.5. The magic number in the PRB is 27: those scoring below it are most likely to possess a wayward impulse and, therefore, may be a poor hiring risk.

How can you increase your score? Just remember that PRB items are measuring self-control and its related subtraits. Low scorers have been found to share similar traits and are often described as selfish, defensive, rebellious, conceited, pessimistic, hard-headed, dissatisfied, bitter, touchy, self-pitying, and moody. High scorers are described as reliable, unselfish, pleasant, cooperative, considerate, patient, good-natured, reasonable, responsible, self-controlled, and industrious. When responding to test items, keep these opposing lists of characteristics in mind. If you can pattern your responses the way a reliable, cooperative, and patient person would, then you should have no trouble passing.

The Hogan Employee Reliability Index (HERI)

The HERI is another personality inventory to emerge from the MMPI/CPI mother lode. As you might expect, the HERI is strikingly similar to the PRB; persons taking both tests wind up with nearly identical scores. In developing their scale, Joyce and Robert Hogan relied upon a popular theory of delinquency which states that people are distributed along a continuum of socialization resembling a bell curve. At the far left are those who are unusually scrupulous and conscientious, in the middle are those who are normally rule-compliant, and at the far right are the lawbreakers who are openly hostile to the rules and conventions of society. Only a few people occupy the extreme positions on this continuum; most of us fall somewhere in the middle.

According to the Hogans, the majority of workplace problems are not caused by the "far righters." They suggest that the real troublemakers come from the ranks of the normally rule-compliant who hide their feelings of anger and frustration. They never let their hostility build to a point where they actually run afoul of the law, but they can easily become an employer's worst nightmare. Such individuals routinely engage in one or more of the following: substance abuse, insubordination, tardiness, absenteeism, excessive grievances, bogus worker-compensation claims, vandalism, and various other forms of passive aggression. The Hogans categorize all these behaviors under the heading of "organizational delinquency."

The organizational delinquent often has another interesting characteristic: charm. Several studies have shown that even the worst offenders usually receive above-average job performance evaluations. This suggests that borderline sociopathic employees may project a nonthreatening/disarming personality toward their supervisors, whereas honest but grumpy employees may be perceived as tolerable annoyances.

The HERI does not respond to charm. It is, however, subject to faking. Once again, we cannot print test items, but they are similar to those found in the section covering the MMPI. An important point to remember when taking the HERI is that it defines delinquency as the product of four basic themes: hostility to rules, thrill-seeking impulsiveness, social insensitivity, and alienation.

1) *Hostility to Rules.* Test items focus on such areas as school success and the degree to which you avoid trouble. Not surprisingly, delinquents usually report poorer grades and several instances of misbehavior.

2) *Thrill-Seeking Impulsiveness.* Delinquents are thought to be thrill seekers. Support for this notion has come from several sources, including a 1982 survey of convenience store workers. When asked why they thought this profession led to such a high rate of employee theft, the third highest response (right behind "pay too low" and "financial need") was "for the thrills/for fun." HERI items check for impulsive-

ness/thrill seeking by asking if you will try anything once, if you enjoy crowds, and if you are exhibitionistic. Responding affirmatively to any of these items will get you points toward delinquency.

3) *Social Insensitivity.* This theme is concerned with the quality of your interpersonal interactions. You can expect to see questions about "likability" (Do you like other people?/Do other people like you?) and about how easy you are to live with.

4) *Alienation:* Test items for this theme will probe general psychological adjustment. To look good, you should report no feelings of depression or anxiety, no undue guilt, and a good sense of attachment and belonging to your peers. As with the PRB, the makers of the HERI describe their low and high scorers. Those passing the test are usually seen as conscientious, attentive to details, modest, and self-confident. They also express a preference for rules, procedures, and structure. You will fail the test if your responses make you look aggressive, hostile, self-indulgent, impulsive, suspicious, and tense.

The Personal Outlook Inventory (POI)

The POI is difficult to categorize because it has features common to both covert and overt integrity tests. At first glance it seems to be an overt test because its purpose, according to the examiner's manual, is to assess the likelihood that an applicant will be "caught stealing cash, merchandise, or other company assets" (Science Research Associates 1987, p.1). This kind of narrow theft criterion is common in traditional overt tests. I've included the POI in this section, however, because it does not contain any overt (e.g., "Do you steal?") items. The makers of the test decided against using obvious references to theft for two reasons: 1) they believe that "Do you steal"-type questions are harshly accusatory and may be offensive to some applicants, and 2) they believe that subtle, covert items are harder to fake.

POI questions are similar in content to those in other tests already discussed. Information is gathered in five areas: personal demographics, general activity level, social and moral values, satisfaction with personal circumstances, and risk-taking behavior. A validity scale is included to check for faking or random responding. These items are just like MMPI validity scale items, but you can only answer five in the scored direction. Any more than that invalidates the test. The only other scale, the S-scale, indicates the probability that you will be fired for stealing. Amazingly, the POI has only 37 items, so you are expected to finish the test in around 15 minutes.

Like the PRB, the POI is designed so that a high score indicates a decreased risk of dishonesty. S-scale items are scored as 0, 1, or 2. If you score from 37 to 50, then you are considered a low-risk applicant. The scoring guide places the probability that you will steal in the future at only 10 percent. Scoring from 33 to 36 makes you a moderate risk, with a 24-percent probability that you will steal. Scoring from 29 to 32 puts you in the substantial risk category, with a 43-percent "future theft" probability. Finally, extreme-risk applicants score between 16 and 28, with a corresponding 57-percent theft probability—this means that the odds are greater than 1 in 2 that these applicants will steal.

Machover Draw-a-Person Test (D-A-P)

Another projective technique. In this test, you will be provided with a pencil and paper and told simply to "draw a person." Upon completion, you will be asked to draw a person of the opposite sex from that of the first figure. While you draw, the examiner will be noting such details as which parts of the body are drawn first (hint: start with the head), and any comments you express. Sometimes the examiner will ask you to make up a story about the people you have drawn. If you aren't specific enough, he/she will prompt you with questions concerning their ages, schooling, occupations, and family life.

The D-A-P scoring guide provides the examiner with detailed instructions on how to prepare a composite personality description. The number of factors that must be evaluated is staggering. Some of the more important ones are the absolute size of the figures; the size of the same-sex figure in relation to the opposite-sex figure; the sizes of various body parts (heads, hands, feet, breasts); the overall quality of the drawing; clothing details; position of arms, legs, and head; orientation of the figures (standing, sitting, running, front or profile view, etc.); background details; and on and on. Leaving nothing to chance, additional instructions cover such possibilities as missing body parts, disproportionate features, shading, and erasures.

Wrestling a clinical interpretation from these figures is more an act of faith than of science. Although the test publishers allude to "thousands of drawings" examined in validation studies, they provide little hard evidence. One critic describes the interpretive guide as a catalog of sweeping generalizations. Some examples: large eyelashes indicate hysteria, many clothing details suggest neurosis, small drawings and/or sad facial expressions indicate depression, few body periphery details (especially fingers) indicate suicidal tendencies, few physical features suggest psychosis, and, the pièce de résistance, a disproportionately large head may indicate an organic brain disease.

When used as an integrity test, the D-A-P places a great deal of emphasis on the relationship between the male and female figures. There is supposedly a tendency for the examinee to project impulses that are acceptable to him or her onto the same-sex figure and impulses that are unacceptable onto the opposite-sex figure. Males, for example, should not make their male figure hostile or openly aggressive. Details to avoid would be an angry, shouting face, clenched fists, arms raised as if to strike, or legs kicking at something. If a story for the figure is required, make it a socially acceptable one. This is not the time to go into a Stephen King mode.

The opposite-sex figure is a different matter. Remember, this figure is said to embody the impulses you wish to avoid. A good story for a male examinee to create for the female figure is that she has just lost her car keys and doesn't know what to do. This shows a disdain for carelessness and weakness/indecisiveness. Another good story would involve the woman trying to get the man to do something that he shouldn't be doing. This can earn a male examinee big points in the integrity department, as long as the man in the story doesn't ultimately acquiesce to her demands.

As you might expect, the validity of D-A-P interpretations is highly controversial. This hasn't stopped others from developing similar tests. One derivative, the House-Tree-Person (H-T-P) Technique, is notable for its interpretations. The clinical diagnosis of the "person" drawing is similar to that found in the D-A-P, but the "tree" drawing is said to be related to the examinee's attitude toward life. A dead tree points to emotional emptiness, a full-blown tree to liveliness, a weeping willow to weakness, and a spiky tree to aggressiveness (really, I'm not making any of this up). Compared to the "person" and "tree" drawings, the "house" drawing has yielded little useful information. The examiner may express concern, however, if you haven't progressed beyond a first-grader's view of a house as a square block with two square windows, a central rectangular door, and a triangle roof.

Handwriting Analysis

I covered handwriting analysis in *Deception Detection* (Paladin Press, 1991), and little has changed since. Despite the continued popularity of this centuries-old technique throughout Europe and the United States, there are still a great many businesses that will not acknowledge their use of it. Why? Perhaps they are afraid of the embarrassment (and lawsuits) that would likely accompany such an announcement. After all, graphology has never proven itself scientifically valid, and the sheer number of contradictory scoring techniques makes it impossible to establish a unified theoretical base. Having your handwriting analyzed is a crapshoot; the outcome is determined to a great extent on the subjective whims of the examiner. About the only useful advice I can give you is to be neat. Neatness seems to be one of the few "positive" characteristics that transcends all the competing schools of thought. Other than that, you're on your own.

* * * * *

A final note. Publishers of covert integrity tests are usually involved in mainstream psychology and often have a long history of producing other, less controversial instruments. Overt test publishers, on the other hand, generally come from the security field and are criticized frequently by their competitors for failing to give proper consideration to the scientific method, statistical analysis, etc. In light of these disparate backgrounds, it is interesting to note that not a single test outlined above has ever been reviewed as an integrity test in the testing industry's definitive sourcebook, the *Mental Measurements Yearbook (MMY)*. The Rorschach, for example, has been reviewed numerous times regarding its role in predicting emotional imbalance, but those studies dealt exclusively with truly disturbed individuals either seeking or receiving psychiatric care. Not once has the Rorschach been reviewed with regard to its purported ability to detect deception. The same holds true for the other personality test warhorse, the MMPI. Why? Probably because most professional researchers don't want to waste time and money just to prove that a perfectly good personality test can be reshaped into something it was not intended to be. Just like you shouldn't use a screwdriver to hammer nails, the argument goes, you shouldn't use a broad-based personality test as a lie detector.

OVERT INTEGRITY TESTS

If we accept the argument that broad-based personality tests are ill-suited to measure integrity, then we can focus our attention on the so-called "overt" methodologies. Initially, personnel psychologists showed little optimism for overt tests because they believed that asking direct personal questions about delinquent behavior would invariably result in faking good, socially desirable answers. Undaunted by this criticism, the military developed an overt test, the Biographical Case History (BCH), to screen inductees deemed unsatisfactory for military service. Some sample BCH items were: "How often do you steal?," "How many of your friends use drugs?," and "Do you consider yourself honest?" Field studies yielded enough favorable results to warrant further research, so a second-generation test was developed for use in the civilian population. This, too, was successful, which led to another version, as well as a name change—the Biographical Case History became the Life Experience Inventory (LEI). Although the LEI continued to produce satisfactory results, its developers withdrew it from the market after only three years due to a concern over potential lawsuits alleging invasion of privacy.

The Reid Report (RR)

John E. Reid and Associates—a giant in the polygraph field—was apparently not as concerned about privacy issues. Their Reid Report picked up where the BCH/LEI left off and is still going strong today. (Interestingly, the RR was not born out of a concern for a more accurate "lie detector." Its presence in the marketplace was a straight business decision: clients who balked at the more costly polygraph screening now had a cheaper alternative.)

The original RR dealt only with theft. The current versions deal with other aspects of dishonesty, as well as alcohol and drug abuse. There's no telling which version of the test you may encounter, but they are all based on the same theoretical framework with its emphasis on attitudes toward theft/dishonesty, biographical information, and admissions of past misbehavior.

Attitudes. Attitudes toward theft are assessed in the first part of the test with approximately 90 yes/no questions.

Some of the items will determine how punitive you are by asking to what extent thievery should be punished. Possible items could be: "Do you believe that stealing from an employer can be condoned if special circumstances exist?" and "If caught stealing, should a trusted, long-term employee be given more leniency than a new hire?" Other questions will probe your overall opinions about theft and honesty, e.g.: "Do you think that you could commit a burglary?" or "Do you consider yourself too honest to steal?"

Biographical Information. The influence of early Biodata tests is clearly seen here. Some items are open-ended, some are yes/no, and some are multiple-choice or biographical completion. These 85 or so questions cover previous employment, education, personal history (e.g., marital status, addresses over the past 10 years), financial history (especially indebtedness), and social history (e.g., use of alcohol and/or drugs, trouble with the law).

Admissions. These are brutally straightforward yes/no questions about your past behavior. Some possible examples are: "Have you, on three or more occasions, written checks knowing that you had insufficient funds to cover them?," and "Have you ever made a false claim to an insurance company?"

The intrusive nature of so many RR items seems to invite faking good responses. Is that the case? Proponents of the test say it is not. Dr. Philip Ash, a former research director for the Reid company, cites the following anecdote to illustrate his point. An applicant for a bank teller's job changed his answer from $600 to $1,000 on the question, "The total amount of money (that did not belong to me) that I have taken from jobs would be about: Can't Remember, None, $1 to $5,000 [in eight increments]." When asked why he had made the change, he gave two reasons: 1) he "knew" that everyone took some money, so he thought the examiner would assume he was lying if he didn't report anything, and 2) he calculated that $1,000 would break down to only about $4 a week for the five years he had been employed. "Doc," he asked, "isn't that par for the course? I want to level with you, and you would think I was some kind of a freak if I said I never took anything!" (Ash, 1971, p. 163). And this is from a guy who wants to be a bank teller!

Lots of people undoubtedly give out way too much information, but that doesn't prove anything about the frequency of faking good responses. A few studies (one of them by Ash) have tried to shed a little more light on the debate. Their basic design goes something like this: RRs (or similar tests) are given first to a group of job applicants and then to a group of known troublemakers—usually prison inmates. It is assumed that the applicants represent the "normal" population and will respond within normal parameters; the prisoners, on the other hand, will presumably try to beat the test by faking good, thus increasing their chances for parole. As expected, the prisoners almost always score significantly lower than the job seekers. Ash and his colleagues take this as evidence that overt tests like the RR are valid and show a strong resistance to faking.

Critics have come to a far different conclusion. Integrity test expert Paul Sackett, for example, calls the "early parole" motive assigned to the prisoners "sheer speculation" (Sakett & Harris 1984, p. 238). Alternative speculative explanations could be: 1) prisoners reasoned faking would lessen their chances of parole, so they responded truthfully; 2) prisoners realized that they would look ridiculous trying to fake good when confronted with questions like, "Most of my coworkers (fellow prisoners) are very honest people," so they responded truthfully; and 3) since anonymity was assured, most prisoners felt no pressure to fake good and instead faked bad to give the researcher what they thought were the desired results.

The question of fakability remains unresolved. No one knows to what extent it occurs, but a group of additional studies has shown that individuals giving socially desirable responses tend to do well on honesty tests. The following hints were culled from these studies:

* *Don't be modest.* One of the questions will ask you to rate your honesty on a five-point scale that ranges from "High Above Average" to "Below Average." Always rate yourself above average or high above average. People who rate themselves average or below usually do worse on the total test.

* *Don't admit to having "thoughts about stealing."* People proven to be dishonest usually report that they think about stealing more often than honest people do.

* *Don't admit to owing large debts.* Although not a measure of honesty per se, people with extraordinary debt loads often get a "Not recommended for employment" evaluation. Reporting frequent changes in jobs and home addresses will also stack the deck against you. Philip Ash states that a middling to high "Recommended" evaluation can still be reversed by a suspicious financial/work history.

* *Don't overestimate.* One question will ask you to estimate the percentage of people who steal from their employers. People who pass the test choose low estimates—10 percent or less. People who fail make estimates in the 30-35 percent (or higher) range.

* *Don't be cynical.* All integrity tests are biased against cynics because of certain assumptions made by the test developers. One of those assumptions is that people who steal/are dishonest think that everybody else steals/is dishonest. This assumption may be correct, but it fails to recognize that other groups—like truly honest cynics—may hold the same opinions. You might be the most honest person in the world, but if you express the belief that lots of people steal from their employers or cheat on their income taxes, then you will fail the test.

* *Don't be lenient.* Another of the test developer's assumptions is that someone who steals will approve of punishment only for those people who steal more than he/she does. Consequently, when you are presented with a "What would you do if . . ." scenario, always recommend strong punishment for any type of dishonesty. If "arrest" is an option, and you know that the behavior described is illegal (no matter how small the crime), then you should choose it.

An interesting case showing the dangers of leniency is outlined by David Lykken in his book *A Tremor in the Blood*. He tells of a woman from Minneapolis who failed a RR questionnaire when applying for a part-time position at B. Dalton Bookstores. Not only did she fail the test, she had the distinction of receiving "the lowest score that they had ever seen" (Lykken 1981, p.238). Most people would be upset upon hearing such news, but this woman had even more reason for concern—she was a nun! Lykken theorizes that this nun, Sister Terressa, was tripped up by her "Christian charity." She almost certainly failed the "punitiveness" items and probably (correctly) viewed the rest of society as less-than-holy, thus decreasing her score on the "attitude toward honesty" items. It is unlikely that she had any damaging admissions, but, if she did, then they drove the final nail into her coffin. The ensuing uproar when Sister Terressa's story went public was a major factor in Minnesota's passing of a statute forbidding polygraph tests, voice stress analyzers, or "any test purporting to test the honesty of an employee or prospective employee."

A few other states have patterned legislation after Minnesota's example, but the Reid Report is still relentlessly marketed—sometimes in less-than-honest ways.

One persistent allegation is that RR salesmen continue to tout their product as the only integrity test reviewed favorably in the eighth edition of the *Mental Measurements Yearbook*, even though the ninth edition contains favorable reviews of other tests (tenth and eleventh editions have since been published). A spokesman for the company responds to this charge as follows: "It's definitely counseled against, and we hope it's avoided" (Bales 1988, p.4).

The newest addition to the Reid's family of tests is a computerized version of the RR. The half-hour program concentrates on past drug abuse and on-the-job theft, and versions of the test have been specifically written for job candidates who will handle money or work in security.

Besides speeding up the administration and scoring of tests, the computer technology allows for a chilling improvement: questions can become more intrusive as the applicant's answers disclose a greater probability of past misbehavior. If you admit, for example, that you have borrowed money from a cash register in the past, the computer can follow up with, "How many times?" or "How much of the borrowed money did you fail to repay?" Brian Jayne, one of the program's developers, states that (surprise, surprise) candidates sometimes hurt their chances by disclosing too much.

The Stanton Survey (SS)

The Stanton Survey is divided into two major sections. The first is comprised of biodata items covering educational and vocational history and social habits. The second part consists of 84 multiple-choice "attitudes" and "admissions" items. Many of the questions have "explain lines" with explicit instructions to provide explanations. An additional sheet of paper is included so that applicants can list their good and bad points as well as the reasons they believe they should be hired.

The Stanton Corporation has also released a "Phase II" version of the SS. It resembles the original version but omits the personal history and biographical information. In addition to the standard scoring and classification guidelines, the SS examiner's manual lists the "seven concepts" on which the test is based. As you might expect, these concepts are practically indistinguishable from the assumptions made by the authors of the RR (e.g., persons who have performed criminal behavior in the past are more likely to display criminal behavior in the future, the attitudes of those who consistently engage in criminal behavior are different from those who refrain from criminal behavior, and criminal behavior is learned primarily through association with those who engage in such behavior). Completed tests are usually scored by computer, resulting in three levels of classification:

1) *Low Risk.* Low-risk applicants have a nonexistent or minimal record of previous dishonest behaviors, particularly when the opportunity to engage in such behavior did exist.

They should not cause any trouble as employees.

2) *Marginal Risk.* These applicants show a consistent enough pattern of dishonesty to make them questionable hires. According to the Stanton Corporation, these individuals should not be trusted in a job situation unless direct supervision is available.

3) *High Risk.* These people have engaged in "recent, severe, and patterned dishonest misbehavior" and should not be placed in a position of trust "under any circumstances" (Ganguli 1985, p. 1470).

The question of fakability seems to be a serious issue with the SS; neither of the test reviewers in the ninth *MMY* are convinced that it can be controlled. Dr. H.C. Ganguli remarks that "the opportunities for faking are numerous" and "the fakability of responses is high" ((Ganguli 1985, pp. 1471-72). He goes on to chide the Stanton Corporation for not investigating this area thoroughly enough. Dr. Kenneth Wheeler's review echoes these sentiments. He sees a "high potential" for faking and even shows how one of Stanton's own studies provides evidence that responses are being faked "in a socially desirable direction" (Wheeler 1985, p. 1473). Both reviewers conclude that the SS suffers from a lack of high-quality validation research.

Because the Reid Report and the Stanton Survey are similar in both theory and item content, the hints described for the RR also apply here. If, however, you should come across an item that you don't know how to answer, just remember the three basic rules of faking good:

1) Never admit to anything serious.

2) Always maintain a punitive attitude.

3) Always express the opinion that your family, friends, and most members of society are honest.

The London House Personnel Selection Inventory (PSI)

The London House PSI is currently available in eight versions measuring everything from honesty and drug avoidance to work values and employee/customer relations. Some versions contain a lengthy survey of personal and employment history (biodata) that can aid in making decisions about borderline candidates. For all versions, test items are presented in a variety of formats, including rating scales, checklists, and open-ended questions.

London House claims that the PSI, introduced in 1975 (24 years after the first Reid Report), is the most widely distributed overt integrity test currently on the market.

This is probably due to London House's astute realization that preemployment polygraph exams were severely limited in their ability to *predict* behavior. Take, for example, a young applicant with no work history. Chances are good that he would easily pass a polygraph exam because he's never had a job-related opportunity to steal. Even experienced employees seem to have little trouble on these preemployment polygraph tests. Why? It's the nature of the beast. Psychologists and security experts have known for years that the polygraph works best when there is an actual crime under investigation. Questions can be drawn directly from the crime scene, and the entire exam can be focused on this one incident. A preemployment interview is conducted under an entirely different set of circumstances. No specific crime is involved, so the test is much more unfocused. Predictions based on these exams are, therefore, tenuous at best. More accurate predictions could be made (in theory at least) if the applicant's cognitive predispositions and propensities could be measured. The polygraph can't do this. London House believes that its PSI can.

Two staunch PSI proponents, John Jones and William Terris, have produced several studies over the years to bolster their enthusiastic claims. They argue that the typical "employee-thief" possesses a number of characteristics easily identifiable with a paper-and-pencil test (notice the similarities to the Reid Report's "assumptions" and the Stanton Survey's "concepts"):

The employee-thief . . .

* often thinks about theft-related activities. Item example:

"In recent years, how many times have you found yourself thinking about taking money without actually doing it?"

* attributes more thefts to others. Example: "How many of your former coworkers do you believe were stealing from their employers?"

* engages in more rationalizations for theft. Example: "I believe that everyone would steal if the conditions were right."

* holds a less punitive attitude toward thieves. Example: "A young employee admitted stealing $50 from her employer. If you were the employer, how would you handle this situation?"

* shows more "inter-thief" loyalty. Example: "If your employer found out that you had been stealing company goods, would you tell on coworkers who had helped you?"

"A typical employee-thief believes he is an 'average' person in a basically dishonest world," say Jones and Terris (1983, p. 187). In reality, however, this kind of person is thought to be more tempted to steal and less able to resist peer pressure than others.

The PSI identifies potential troublemakers through an elaborate scoring system. First, a raw score is derived for each scale. These raw scores are then transformed into more meaningful percentile, risk category, and low-risk confidence scores. A typical PSI measuring dishonesty, violence, and drug abuse would therefore generate nine scores. Here's what the three transformed scores mean:

1) *Percentile*. A straightforward ranking of the applicant in question with the rest of the test-taking population. Scores are reported as percentiles so that the examiner can see the exact percentage of people who have scored above and below the applicant.

2) *Risk Category*. Rates the applicant as either low-, borderline-, or high-risk based on past behavior. The breakdown of the six-point honesty scale is: low-risk (1-2),

"Applicant has no significant history of theft-related offenses"; borderline-risk (3-4), "Applicant has a recent history of theft behavior"; high-risk (5-6), "Applicant has a current history of theft behavior involving significant amounts of money, merchandise, etc." (Jones & Terris 1983, p.188).

3) *Low Risk Confidence*. Predicts the probability that the applicant will avoid future problems in this area. Scores range from 1-100, with a higher score meaning a greater probability that the applicant is a low risk. One additional score of some use is the total number of items omitted. According to the test publishers, people have a tendency to skip items that directly incriminate them. Really honest people are thought to answer all questions; dishonest people are thought to skip items because they have something to hide.

Even though the PSI has shown some favorable results (and, to its credit, several studies have been published in mainstream peer-reviewed journals), there are still nagging doubts as to whether it can predict "integrity" reliably. Two studies serve as illustration. In the first, the PSI's effectiveness was tested by hiring a large number (527) of department store workers regardless of their preemployment PSI scores. Of the 32 employees who were subsequently discharged for theft or other offenses, 28 had failed the test. What's more, mean honesty scale scores for those discharged were significantly lower than for those not discharged. So far, these results look pretty promising.

Unfortunately, the dark cloud overshadowing all this good news is that 342 of the remaining 495 employees not discharged had also failed the test. Remember, under normal circumstances, these 342 productive and seemingly honest workers would not have been hired. The authors of the study don't seem too surprised or concerned by such a high number of false positives. Instead, they assert that many of those with failing scores were probably stealing significant amounts of money and/or merchandise and just hadn't been caught yet. This assumption is, of course, absolutely impossible to prove.

The second study involved 80 minimum-wage "kettlers" hired by the Salvation Army to work eight-hour shifts ringing a bell to solicit Christmas donations. Once again the PSI was administered at time of hire but not used in the hiring decision. Average daily intake served as a rough measure of honesty, and, to eliminate one area of bias, the kettlers were assigned to areas previously documented as low-, medium-, and high-profit locations. At first glance, the results again looked promising: the average daily intake was $81 for those recommended by the test and $62.77 for those not recommended. Is this evidence that the low scorers were stealing from their kettles? The researchers seemed to think so. Critics, however, charge that other possible explanations were overlooked. Some of the kettlers may have taken unauthorized breaks (an undesirable behavior to be sure, but not in the same league as stealing). Also, physical attractiveness and differences in solicitation techniques were not considered, even though it seems reasonable to assume that a pretty, cheerful girl would collect more donations than a scruffy, sullen man. Failure to acknowledge these and other possible extenuating factors greatly diminishes the credibility of the conclusions the researchers put forth. Like other tests before it, the London House PSI remains a controversial measure of employee honesty.

The Phase II Profile

The Phase II Profile has three components: the Integrity Status Inventory (ISI), which is the main "honesty test" for preemployment screening; an ADdendum (AD), which elicits information about drug and alcohol abuse; and an In-House Security Survey (IHSS), which serves as an honesty test for current employees. Because it is not used for preemployment purposes, the IHSS will not be discussed here.

The 116-item ISI contains true/false and multiple-choice items in six content categories: ability to rationalize dishonesty, how often a person thinks or plans about doing something dishonest, basic honest attitudes, basic dishonest attitudes, dishonesty admissions, and a lie scale. Not surprisingly, the bulk of the test items comes from the honest/dishonest attitudes scales and the admissions scale. The lie scale is unique in that each item represents a 10-percent differential in the total "faking" score. Only if you answer all 10 questions "correctly" (as determined by the test developers) will you be categorized as giving 100-percent truthful responses. Answering nine of them correctly amounts to a "90-percent truthful attempt," and so on. Combining scores from all these scales yields a total score. Total scores greater than 147 are said to be characteristic of those who commit theft. A score of less than 140 indicates honesty. The gray area between 140 and 147 equates roughly to an "inconclusive" score on a polygraph.

The AD is much shorter than the ISI and is composed entirely of admissions items. Several questions ask how many times you have purchased, sold, or used (both on and off the job) a variety of drugs; additional questions ask how recently you have engaged in such behaviors. Alcohol use and abuse is similarly covered.

Faking a good score on the AD would seem to be a cakewalk, especially after seeing some of the laughably improbable response alternatives. A typical example exploring the number of missed work days due to intoxication has responses ranging from "refuse [to answer]" to "daily" to "I lost count." Would anyone really be stupid enough to choose one of these alternatives? Apparently so. Phase II's Gregory Lousig-Nont says that they get a "surprising number" of admissions about drug and alcohol use. He goes on to describe these questions as superior even to urine analysis because "there won't be a false positive with paper-and-pencil tests" (Gavzer 1990, p.5).

As overt tests go, the Phase II Profile is hardly distinguishable from the Reid, Stanton, or London House versions. All are based on similar premises, all have similar test items, and all have a similar scoring rationale. The Phase II, however, has become the target of extreme—even hostile—criticism.

One psychologist, University of Illinois professor Benjamin Kleinmuntz, seems barely able to contain his disgust with the instrument. He attacks the Phase II Profile on several fronts, leaving little doubt as to his opinion of its effectiveness.

On test score interpretation:

> . . . No evidence supporting these interpretive claims, or how interpretations were determined, nor the score values accompanying such claims appear in the research literature. But more importantly, nowhere do they provide evidence in the accompanying manual, "Statistical Validation Report." This is a clear violation of the EEOC Guidelines . . . (*MMY* 10 p. 636).

On validation studies conducted by the publisher:

> [In the first study] absolutely no validity information is provided, which possibly goes unnoticed by most prospective users (e.g., lawyers, personnel managers) because reliability and validity are commonly confused with one another (p. 636).

The second and third publisher-sponsored studies do provide validity information, but Kleinmuntz is unimpressed with their results because they do nothing more than compare ISI scores with highly infallible polygraph tests. Integrity test expert Paul Sackett is also critical of these two studies and points out that the third has artificially inflated correlations due to poor experimental design.

On adverse-impact studies conducted by the publisher:

Kleinmuntz calls these studies "nonsense" because of their poor design. The publishers nonetheless provide a letter from a law office in their marketing literature which seeks

to assure potential customers that the Phase II does not discriminate on the basis of race, sex, or age. Kleinmuntz
believes this letter to be "seriously misleading" because "the
test scores and the arbitrary test score cutting points for honesty versus dishonesty were not properly validated—at least
not according to any of the [American Psychological
Association's] "Standards for Educational and Psychological
Testing" (p. 638).

On the Addendum:

> It is useless . . . not a shred of evidence is pre-
> sented regarding [its] standardization, reliability, or
> validity. But this does not deter the distributors
> from interpreting the meaning of various scores
> and of warning employees to "exercise caution in
> considering this person for employment" when
> certain scores are achieved . . . (pp. 636-37).

On the Phase II Profile as a whole:

> No corporate user should waste money and time
> denying employment on the basis of this question-
> able tool, and no person should be denied the
> opportunity for a job on the basis of scores from this
> instrument. It is my contention that it is illegal and
> unethical to do so in the case of minority or protect-
> ed class applicants, and it is unethical and uncon-
> scionable to do so in all other instances (p. 638).

That's pretty rough stuff. Fortunately, the Phase II Profile
is no harder to fake than any of the other overt tests—the
same previously covered rules apply to all of them. And
even if you do fail it, you could still benefit in the long run.
How? By contacting a lawyer. If Kleinmuntz's charges are
correct, then the Phase II Profile is a lawsuit waiting to happen. Now I know that's a pretty drastic step, but I can guar-

antee you that someone will eventually take on an overt test the way Sibi Soroka has challenged the MMPI. Of course no one knows what the outcome of such a court action would be, but the odds seem to be with the plaintiff—especially if the plaintiff is a member of a minority or other protected class. And, as an added bonus, you could probably get the whole ball rolling at no cost just by contacting the ACLU. They have offices in every state.

* * * * *

Throughout this chapter, I have tried to remain focused on two areas: 1) how integrity tests have failed to achieve the minimum standards for scientific respectability and 2) how specific knowledge of these tests can lead to improved scores. As for the latter—the "hints," if you will—I hope I have provided enough information to keep you from scoring as poorly as Sister Terressa. The first area, unfortunately, has been dealt with briefly and in broad strokes—space limitations prohibit a detailed technical discussion of how tests are developed and refined. In closing, however, I would like to outline a few of the scientific (and ethical) problems surrounding integrity tests.

The Scientific Argument against Integrity Tests

In order to determine the effectiveness of an integrity test (or any test, for that matter), the developer must conduct a series of validation studies. These studies can differ greatly in their methods, but they are all designed to get at the truth (i.e., can the test do what it claims to be able to do). Integrity test researchers have used approximately five different validation strategies, each of which is flawed. First, integrity tests scores were compared with polygraph judgments. These studies attempted to show that poor honesty scores would invariably coincide with poor performance on the polygraph. Although the relationship was not perfect, there emerged strong evidence that the two techniques provided similar results. The problem, of course, is that the polygraph is just as controversial as its paper-and-pencil counterpart. As Sackett and Harris (1984) put it, "A criterion which is seriously questioned in the scientific community cannot serve as the basis for meaningful evaluation of new instruments, such as honesty tests" (p. 241).

A second approach, already mentioned with regard to the Reid Report, is to compare the test scores of two groups—one presumably dishonest (prisoners are the obvious choice) and one presumed to represent the general population. These "contrasted group" studies are hopelessly flawed from the outset due to their reliance upon unproven assumptions made about each group (e.g., prisoners will always try to fake good).

The third strategy defines validity as a high correlation between admissions items and attitude items. The theory here is that people who admit a significant number of past misbehaviors will also score poorly on the attitude items, thus proving that attitude items alone are able to differentiate between the honest and the dishonest.

Remember, however, that the converse must also be taken into account: people who admit fewer past misbehaviors will probably perform better on the attitude items. That's the problem. Most researchers agree that integrity tests tend to elicit socially desirable responses: admissions are curtailed and attitudes are distorted in a positive direction. Correlations in such studies are always artificially inflated and do not serve as very compelling evidence.

The fourth approach uses what is known as a "time series design," the most common of which proceeds through three phases: 1) a store is selected and monitored so that a baseline level of shrinkage can be determined, 2) an honesty testing program is instituted, and 3) after a period of time, shrinkage levels can be checked again. The program is said to be successful (valid) if shrinkage rates go down after its implementation. Judging by the marketing literature, this design is exceedingly popular with integrity test publishers.

Only rarely does a brochure fail to describe a glowing recommendation from some hapless manager whose store was turned around after the integrity test was introduced. "We're amazed," they usually say. "We've reduced our shrinkage 40 percent in the past month alone. Thank you, thank you, thank you!"

Although impressive, such testimonials have little to do with the actual validity of a test. The question is one of causality: is shrinkage going down because more honest employees are being hired, or is it going down because of a perceived increase in organizational concern about employee theft? The latter is certainly a credible alternative, one of many. Others include seasonal variations, management changes, and fluctuations in the economy. To date, no time series design reported in the professional journals has had enough control over the organizational environment to prove that the test was the sole cause of shrinkage reduction. There has always been room for unrelated factors to bias the results.

The final validation strategy is the most commonsensical but also hardest to accomplish. It begins by giving all potential job candidates an integrity test and then hiring them regardless of their scores. After some time has passed, these new employees are rated (usually by their immediate superior) to see how well their test scores predicted their on-the-job performance. Of special interest are those individuals who have actually been caught stealing; researchers can then review their test scores to see if they would have provided a warning.

These predictive studies would generate the most compelling evidence for the effectiveness of integrity tests, but so far they have suffered from the fact that the number of employee-thieves who have actually been caught is scant. Testing proponents don't see this as a serious drawback because, even though their numbers are small, the people who are caught almost always have poor test scores. Therefore, they say, the test has proved itself useful. Testing critics disagree. They point out that huge numbers of individuals routinely fail these tests (some failure rates are as high as 75 percent), but the majority of them are neither caught nor suspected of stealing. Such a high false-positive rate is, to say the least, discomforting.

As of this writing, no major developments in integrity test validity have been reported. The debate between proponents and critics continues, of course, but the situation remains about the same as it was in 1990 when the Congressional Office of Technology Assessment released a report entitled "The Use of Integrity Tests for preemployment Screening." Under the heading "Quality of Research," the OTA issued this "finding":

> Given the paucity of independent confirmation of research results, problems identified in published reviews and in OTA's review of a sample of validity studies, and unresolved problems relating to the definition and measurement of the underlying psychological constructs, OTA finds that the existing research is insufficient as a basis for supporting the assertion that these tests can reliably predict dishonest behavior in the workplace. (p. 10).

The Ethical Argument against Integrity Tests

While acknowledging that business owners have a right to protect themselves from counterproductive and criminally inclined employees, integrity test critics question whether these paper-and-pencil confessionals are fair to the vast majority of honest job applicants. One persistent criticism focuses attention on the actual test items: they are flawed, it is argued, because they are based on unproven assumptions. A passing score cannot be achieved unless the applicant demonstrates a punitive and authoritarian attitude; leniency is unacceptable, even though there is no hard evidence linking a charitable disposition to dishonesty. Admissions items—equally unsupported—also give rise to some devilish catch-22s and logical conundrums: If Applicant A honestly reports his past misbehaviors, then he is penalized with a lower test score. Applicant B, on the other hand, can withhold equally damaging information about his past and obtain a higher score—thus being rewarded for lying. As far as the integrity test is concerned, the applicant who tries to turn his life around and plot a course on the straight-and-narrow is deemed less trustworthy than the applicant who continues to lie. This kind of twisted logic should be reason enough to cast doubts on the predictive capabilities of attitudes/admissions items, but there's more: these items consistently fail to take into account the strong role that situational variables play in determining behavior. The trait-heavy nature of most integrity tests is indefensible against what many see as fundamentally a security or "environment management" problem.

Whether or not integrity test items are based on an ill-conceived theory of honesty is still hotly debated by opposing camps of psychologists and professional researchers. Other groups—like civil libertarians—are more concerned with privacy issues raised by the tests. Where is the line drawn between information an applicant would like to keep private and information an employer would like to factor into the hiring decision? That is a difficult question. Test publishers take the position that their questions are not unduly invasive, and, as evidence, they refer to studies which show that most job applicants seem to take it all in stride. In one study, only 11 percent agreed that this type of questionnaire was an invasion of privacy, while 69 percent disagreed. When asked if they resented such a questionnaire, only 3 percent responded affirmatively. Unfortunately, these results are far from conclusive. There is a strong probability that many of the applicants did not want to hurt their chances for employment by maligning the test, so they stuck with the socially desirable response. (Interestingly, this kind of "self-protecting" instinct may have helped them more than they realized: additional studies have shown that those who object more to an integrity test are more likely to receive lower scores.)

Despite the claims of the test publishers, it seems likely

that the overall rate of dissatisfaction is much higher than 3 percent. One need only look at the number of complainants who signed onto Sibi Soroka's MMPI lawsuit to realize that these tests are not just invasive—they are downright offensive. They contain gross intrusions into sensitive areas, and, more importantly, they show little regard for an individual's dignity and self-esteem. Nowhere is this more evident than in the way they lump the entire job-seeking population into two categories: "recommended for hire," and "not recommended for hire."

Discovering that you had been denied employment due to a poor test score would be bad enough if it happened only once, but what if there are long-term repercussions? Two possibilities exist. In the first, your score could find its way into some kind of labor pool data base much in the same way your financial history now resides in one (or more) of the three giant credit-reporting firms. Second, if integrity tests are found to be sufficiently reliable—not valid, just reliable—then their use could lead to a burgeoning population of individuals who are systematically denied employment due to their constant failures. Both of these scenarios would result in the establishment of a permanent score-derived underclass: applicants unable to find work because of their inability to jump through the correct integrity test hoops. Is this fair?

I don't think so, and I know that many, many other people feel the same way. A paper-and-pencil integrity test will never be ethically defensible until it can prove its scientific validity, and that doesn't appear to be anywhere on the horizon. Benjamin Kleinmuntz may have put it best when he said:

> [They] are on the same shaky ground as are the polygraphs against which they were validated, and are the equivalent of a random procedure. Individuals may just as well use a lottery because both methods randomly and unfairly deny persons access to certain jobs on the basis of irrelevant and flawed

information. In that sense they are themselves dishonest devices. They are dishonest towards employers because they reject many potentially productive workers, hence causing greater costs than savings. And they are dishonest toward prospective employees because they constitute an unfair method of screening. (Kleinmuntz 1989, p. 638).

CHAPTER FOUR

PRACTICE TEST

To say that paper-and-pencil tests can deny someone the right to a livelihood is true.

—London House's
Sam Maurice (1990)

No adequate data-base now exists to support the use of honesty tests.

—The American Psychological Association's Committee on Psychological Tests and Assessments (1988)

Now it's time to see how much helpful integrity test information you have retained. What follows is a copy of the Preemployment Integrity Evaluation (PEIE), and this is the only place you'll ever see it. Designed as a realistic copy of actual integrity tests, the PEIE contains multiple-choice, yes/no, and true/false questions covering a wide range of counterproductive behaviors. A lie scale is also included to counter the faking of good responses. Overt items make up a majority of the test, but a few covert personality-type queries have been slipped in for their additional probative value.

To take the test, find a nice, quiet place where you won't be disturbed, read each item carefully, and circle the appropriate response. Unlike with "real" integrity tests, you won't be penalized for leaving a question blank. You should try to answer them all, however, because the scoring instructions will show you whether your response would have helped you or hurt you on an actual test.

About the scoring—the instructions may look imposing at first, but this was necessary to mimic more precisely the way popular integrity tests are scored. Such detail, complex though it may be, gives you an invaluable inside view of how a test is broken down into individual scales and subscales. As long as you pay attention to what you are doing, you should have no trouble scoring and interpreting your results. Keep in mind, however, that this test has no reliability or validity data, and the risk categories and recommendations are totally unsupported. The PEIE is meant to be a teaching tool—a practice run, if you will. So don't take any score you may receive too seriously.

Are you ready? Then go ahead and begin. Good luck!

THE PREEMPLOYMENT INTEGRITY EVALUATION

1. I believe that most of my friends are super honest. T / F

2. There are times when I like to get away from everything and be by myself. T / F

3. I would be upset if a friendly coworker was fired for taking home a box of paper clips. Y / N

4. I occasionally like to have an alcoholic drink at break-fast. T / F

5. As a child, I was never punished for misbehaving. T / F

6. Have you ever destroyed company property in a fit of anger? Y / N

7. It is impossible to be totally honest. T / F

8. There are times when I just can't seem to get going. T / F

9. An employer discovers that a worker has been remov-ing aluminum drink cans from a recycling bin so that he may cash them in on the way home. What action should be taken against him?
    Ignored / Warned / Suspended / Fired / Arrested

10. I think some crimes are so awful that they require a death penalty. Y / N

11. Have you ever consumed alcohol while on the job? Y / N

12. I have laughed occasionally at a dirty or racist joke. T / F

13. If someone has hurt me, I'll make sure that I get even. T / F

14. Most people will speak up if they are given too much change by a cashier. T / F

15. I sometimes have thoughts that I wouldn't want my supervisor to know about. T / F

16. An employee who takes home damaged merchandise without permission should be treated just as if the merchandise were not damaged. Y / N

17. I believe that the fear of being caught keeps most people honest. T / F

18. How many times a week do you use marijuana? Don't Use / 1-2 / 3-4 / 5-7 / More than 7

19. I always tell the truth. T / F

20. If I knew a coworker was stealing company property, I would probably keep my mouth shut. T / F

21. I think that the typical supervisor works just as hard as his/her subordinates. T / F

22. Like most people, I have occasionally broken a minor traffic law. T / F

23. I really don't think that a lot of people cheat on their income tax. T / F

24. When was the last time you used cocaine, crack, or any other illegal drug? Never Used / Over 5 Yrs. Ago / 1-5 Yrs. Ago This Year / This Month / This Week

25. Have you ever stolen something because you were short on cash at the time? Y / N

26. Most employers treat their workers fairly. T / F

27. Do you blush easily? Y / N

28. I can recall at least one instance in my life when I "got away" with something. T / F

29. Sometimes I have been too hung over to perform my job adequately. T / F

30. Have you ever tried to defraud a coworker or an employer? Y / N

31. Cheating a little on an expense account is a common occurrence. T / F

32. Most job-related accidents can't be avoided. T / F

33. Have you ever used a company Xerox machine without permission? Y / N

34. I have smoked marijuana while on the job. T / F

35. Would you cover up an act of vandalism to keep a coworker out of trouble? Y / N

36. There are some special circumstances that would excuse a minor act of theft. T / F

37. Compared with others, how honest are you?
Well Above Avg. / Above Avg. / Avg. / Below Avg. / Well Below Avg.

38. I think that the business owners break more laws than the workers. T / F

39. Would you gamble on a sure thing? Y / N

40. As a rule, I almost always try to give people a second chance. Y / N

41. How many times a week do you use cocaine, crack, or any other illegal drug?
Don't Use / 1-2 / 3-4 / 5-7 / More than 7

42. I sometimes hated my parents when I was growing up. T / F

43. Have you ever stolen something even though you had the money to pay for it? Y / N

44. The average person will sneak into a movie theater if he/she knows that the chances of being caught are very small. T / F

45. I'm not good at expressing love or caring emotions. T / F

46. If you were the boss, would you treat a long-term employee differently from a new hire if both were caught punching the time clock for friends? Y / N

47. Have you ever sold marijuana? Y / N

48. There have been times in my life when I thought about suicide. T / F

49. Would you damage company property if you thought a supervisor was treating you unfairly? Y / N

50. I wouldn't be surprised if half the workers in the United States occasionally took home small things from their employers. T / F

51. Do you often feel embarrassed? Y / N

52. Do you think that a person should be treated like a criminal if she steals something her family really needs? Y / N

53. Everybody has a little dishonesty in them. T / F

54. What would you estimate to be the total amount of money and/or merchandise that you have taken from previous employers?
Less than $10 / $10-$100 / $101-$500 / $501-$1,000 / Over $1,000

55. I have used cocaine, crack, or other illegal drugs while on the job. T / F

56. I believe that the typical supervisor obeys the rules he/she sets for others. T / F

57. I have never used profanity. T / F

58. Have you ever punched a friend's time card when he/she wasn't at work? Y / N

59. Taking a pen home from work is stealing. T / F

60. I sometimes feel inferior or insignificant. T / F

61. An employer discovers that a worker occasionally smokes marijuana on the job. What action should be taken against the worker?
Ignored / Warned / Suspended / Fired / Arrested

62. I believe in the phrase "An eye for an eye and a tooth for a tooth." Y / N

63. I have come to work intoxicated on more than one occasion. T / F

64. I have never gotten angry at anyone. T / F

65. Have you ever faked an injury to collect money from an insurance company? Y / N

66. The average person will think about stealing something if he/she really wants it. T / F

67. I am not the most prompt person in the world. T / F

68. When was the last time you used marijuana?
Never Used / Over 5 Yrs. Ago / 1-5 Yrs. Ago
This Year / This Month / This Week

69. I always feel happy. T / F

70. Have you ever gotten a friend to punch your time card when you were not at work? Y / N

71. I am too honest to steal. T / F

72. I get upset when things don't go my way. T / F

73. If I were the boss, I'd be more apt to overlook a minor incident of shoplifting if the employee were a single mother. Y / N

74. Have you ever sold cocaine, crack, or any other illegal substance? Y / N

75. I have never done anything for which I've later felt ashamed. T / F

SCORING

Lie Scale

Give yourself 1 point for each of these items that you answered T:
5, 19, 57, 64, 69, 75
Put this total at A _____.

Give yourself 1 point for each of these items that you answered F:
12, 28, 42, 48
Put this total at B _____.

Add A and B. If this total is 5 or less, proceed to the next section. If this total is 6 or greater, you have failed the test due to an overwhelming suspicion that you have either responded randomly or have not answered the questions candidly. You are *not recommended for hire.*
A _____ + B _____ = _____ lie scale score.

Attitudes

Punitive Subscale

Give yourself 1 point for each of these items that you answered Y:
3, 40, 46, 73
Put this total at A _____.

Give yourself 1 point for each of these items that you answered N: 10, 16, 52, 62
Put this total at B _____.

For multiple-choice questions 9 and 61, give yourself 1 point each if you chose any alternative except Fired or Arrested.
Put this total at C _____.

Add A, B, and C. This is your punitiveness score _____.

General Honesty Subscale

Give yourself 1 point for each of these items that you answered T:

7, 17, 31, 32, 36, 38, 44, 50, 53, 66

Put this total at D _____

Give yourself 1 point for each of these items that you answered F:

1, 14, 21, 23, 26, 56, 59, 71

Put this total at E _____.

Add D and E. This is your general honesty score _____.

Add your punitiveness score to your general honesty score to get your attitudes scale score. Compare this score to the guide below to see if you are a low-, medium-, or high-risk job candidate based upon your attitudes.

A _____ + B _____ + C _____ = _____ punitiveness score.
D _____ + E _____ = _____ general honesty score.
attitudes scale score _____.

0-7 = low risk.
8-14 = medium risk.
Over 14 = high risk.

Admissions

Give yourself 1 point for each of these items that you answered T or Y:

2, 8, 15, 22, 27, 33, 39, 45, 51, 60, 67, 72

Put this total at A _____.

Give yourself 4 points for each of these items that you answered T or Y:

6, 13, 20, 25, 30, 35, 43, 49, 58, 65, 70

Put this total at B._____.

Give yourself 4 points for question 37 if you chose any alternative except Above Avg. or Well Above Avg.
Put this total at C _____.

Give yourself 4 points for question 54 if you chose any alternative except Less than $10.
Put this total at D _____.

Add A, B, C, and D. This is your admissions scale score. Compare this score to the guide below to see if you are a low-, medium-, or high-risk job candidate based upon your admissions.

A _____ + B _____ + C _____ + D _____ = _____ admissions scale score.

0-8 = low risk.
9-20 = medium risk.
Over 20 = high risk.

Drug/Alcohol Use

Give yourself 1 point for each of these items that you answered T or Y:
4, 11, 29, 34, 47, 55, 63, 74
Put this total at A _____.

For multiple-choice questions 18 and 41, give yourself 1 point each if you chose any alternative except Don't Use.
Put this total at B _____.

For multiple-choice questions 24 and 68, give yourself 1 point each if you chose any alternative except Never Used.
Put this total at C _____.

Add A, B, and C. This is your drug/alcohol use scale score. Compare this score to the guide below to see if you are a low-, medium-, or high-risk job candidate based upon your drug/alcohol use.

A _____ + B _____ + C _____ = _____ drug/alcohol use scale score.

0 = low risk.
1-2 = medium risk.
Over 2 = high risk.

RECOMMENDATIONS

Scoring high on any of the scales = *Not recommended for hire.*

Scoring medium on two or more scales = *Not recommended for hire.*

Scoring low on all scales – or – scoring two lows and one medium = *Recommended for hire.*

INTEGRITY TESTS DOS AND DON'TS

DO take these tests seriously. Your potential employers do.

DON'T get overly imaginative on projective tests like the Rorschach. What you might consider creative may be viewed as bizarre.

DON'T admit to risk-taking behavior. It is a fairly well-established indicant of delinquency/dishonesty.

DON'T admit to "thinking about" theft.

DO pattern your responses to make yourself look conventional, responsible, and self-controlled.

DON'T give answers that make you look rebellious, defensive, or moody.

DON'T hesitate to choose the socially desirable response, even if that's not how you really feel. Studies have shown that people who fake good get better scores. So, if asked to rate your level of honesty, always choose Above Average or Well Above Average.

DON'T admit to owing large debts or to anything else that might make your financial/work history look suspicious.

DON'T mistake intelligence for "street smarts." The former has been shown to be of no help at all on an integrity test. The latter is unquestionably of more benefit.

DO finish the test quickly. If your examiner is also responsible for test scoring and evaluation, he/she may factor in his/her subjective opinions when making a hiring recommendation. Dawdling through a test can be interpreted as anxiety or as an attempt at faking, so it should be avoided.

DO answer every question even if you consider some of them intrusive or offensive. A blank item is interpreted as a deliberate attempt to avoid an area that hits a little too close to home.

DO question the examiner about the test's reliability and validity coefficients. At the very least, this alerts him/her to the fact that you know a little something about test theory.

DO ask to see your score. Most tests have multiple cut-offs depending on the needs of the company. If your score falls into a borderline area, then the examiner might be willing to give you the benefit of the doubt—especially if you've already expressed a certain degree of knowledge about integrity tests.

DO take the practice test. It's an easy and (hopefully) enjoyable way to find out how you might fare on an actual test.

DON'T assume that failing a test makes you a bad person. Integrity test misclassification rates are notoriously high. Remember, as many as 75 percent of all applicants will fail certain tests, and one test apparently had such high standards that not even a nun could pass it.

DO learn your legal rights. If you feel that you have been unjustly denied employment due to an integrity test, then contact the ACLU or see a lawyer. The overwhelming majority of testing authorities agree that no single test score should serve as the sole basis for a hiring decision.

DON'T be afraid to speak up for your rights. If you don't do it, nobody else will.

FINALLY, THE BIG 3

DO express a rosy world view, e.g., "All my friends are honest," "Most of society is honest," etc. Cynicism will kill you!

DO express a punitive attitude. If you are given a choice of punishments, always choose the harshest.

DON'T EVER admit anything of consequence.

RELIABILITY VERSUS VALIDITY: A PRIMER

Despite the efforts of reformers to improve the credibility of the integrity test industry, aggressive marketers continue to capitalize on the layman's confusion with reliability and validity. In fact, it's quite likely that most company-based examiners have no idea of the profound differences that separate these two most basic testing concepts. This is especially true for smaller businesses that lack the resources to keep a qualified testing expert on staff. Not knowing any better, these small business owners can be wowed by a salesman's rapid-fire delivery laced with breathless references to .9 alphas, low error coefficients, and significant Pearson Product Moment Correlations. This statistical assault may lead to a sale, but far too often the purchaser has no idea if the test publisher can adequately support the claims made in its glossy brochures. At the very least, anyone relying on a test score for something as important as a hiring decision should know how the test has proven itself reliable and how the test has proven itself valid. As you'll see below, these two terms are not as easily defined as some might lead you to believe.

RELIABILITY

To understand reliability, you must first understand what is known as the "classical theory of test scores." It begins with the assumption that all tests are imperfect: no matter how well constructed a test may be, it will always fall prey to a certain amount of measurement error. Consequently, the score you receive on any test is not your "true" score; it is instead an "observed" score which can be thought of as the best estimate of your true abilities that can be made from an imperfect instrument. The standard equation is:

$$X = T + E$$

Where X is the observed score, T is the true score, and E is the error. Reliability is concerned only with E—the measurement error. Put simply, the fundamental difference between a high-reliability test and a low-reliability test is the amount of measurement error that creeps into each one.

Historically, these reliability estimates have been derived using three methods: test-retest, parallel forms, and internal consistency.

Test-retest reliability. Used when a researcher wants to see how well a test performs over time. The typical procedure is to administer the test, wait a predetermined amount of time (an hour, a day, a week, etc.), and then administer the exact same test to the exact same people.

Reliability is defined as the correlation between these two scores: the higher the correlation, the higher the reliability. The problem, as you may have guessed, is that these correlations tend to be inflated—especially when the intervening time period is short.

Parallel forms reliability. With this method, two versions of a test are constructed according to the same rules, but each version has different items. In theory, as long as both sets of items are similar in form, content, and degree of difficulty, then both tests should measure the same attribute. Once again, the correlation between these two sets of scores is used as an estimate of reliability. This method is probably the best of the three at assessing reliability, but, because of the difficulty and cost inherent in constructing two parallel tests, it is rarely used.

Internal consistency. This method is the obvious choice for researchers who don't want to get involved with parallel forms. Instead of creating two different tests, a single test is treated as if it were two by grouping the items into two equal halves. A reliability coefficient is then obtained by comparing the scores on each half. Although pitting the even-numbered questions against the odds is the most straightforward way of "splitting halves," other alternatives exist, e.g., top versus bottom, first and third quarters versus second and last quarters, etc. The question then becomes one of which splitting to use because each can result in a slightly different reliability figure. This problem can be—and usually is—sidestepped through a bit of statistical wizardry known as the Kuder-Richardson method: a mathematical formula that automatically averages all the reliability estimates for every possible way in which the items could be split. Such a procedure yields a quite accurate reliability estimate.

Understanding how reliability coefficients are obtained should lead you to the obvious follow-up question: how high should it be before it's high enough? Since the coefficient can range from .00 (totally unreliable) to 1.00 (perfect reliability), it has been suggested that estimates in the range of .70 to .80 are good enough for most purposes in basic research. Integrity tests, however, should be held accountable to a higher standard. Testing experts Robert Kaplan and Dennis Saccuzzo argue that "when tests are used to make important decisions about someone's future you must be certain to minimize any error in classification" (1982, p. 106). They believe that a .95 reliability coefficient is not an unreasonable demand. Unfortunately, very few (if any) integrity tests have reached this goal.

VALIDITY

The unadulterated definition of validity is the degree to which a test measures what it is designed to measure. Like reliability, however, validity is a multifaceted concept. Different types and subcategories and definitions have appeared over the years, each one claiming to describe the true nature of validity. Only since 1974 has there been an agreement by the majority of testing researchers to set aside their differences in favor of a standardized three-heading classification system. Those headings are content, criterion-related, and construct.

Content validity. (A test that is content valid is said to possess an adequate representation of the conceptual domain it is supposed to cover.) If you were to take an algebra test, for example, but the examiner had thrown in a number of questions about the Civil War, then the test would have poor content validity.

Criterion-related validity. This type of validity tells how well a test score relates to a predefined measure of the concept in question. Integrity tests, for example, have two popular criterion measures: future job performance and actual workplace theft. If you were to score poorly on an integrity test (but were hired anyway) and were later found with a car trunk full of your employer's office supplies, then that integrity test would have shown good criterion-related validity. Not surprisingly, integrity test publishers love a high criterion-related validity because that allows them to promote their test as having crystal-ball-like predictive capabilities.

Construct validity. Construct validity is a painstaking study of the adequacy of a test as a measure of a specified psychological construct. And what is a construct? It is an idea or a concept that does not lend itself well to an easily definable set of characteristics. "Intelligence" is a construct, because no one can say for certain what it actually is. "Love" is another construct, as is "honesty" and its close synonym "integrity."

The nebulous nature of constructs makes it difficult to ascertain whether or not a test has construct validity. The most popular approach is to see how well one test correlates with other tests that are believed to measure the same construct. This is called the "convergent evidence" method because a group of highly correlated tests are thought to be converging or narrowing in on the same thing. As I mentioned earlier, the Personnel Reaction Blank and the Hogan Employee Reliability Index yield strikingly similar scores; they can therefore be said to possess a certain degree of construct validity for the construct of "integrity." A great deal more evidence is needed, though, before we can be sure that the popular integrity tests are really measuring "integrity."

One final type of validity, *face validity*, does not fit in with the categories above. Instead of relying upon hard, scientifically derived evidence, face validity amounts to nothing more than a gut reaction: if a test "looks like" it should work, then it has face validity. As far as integrity tests are concerned, the overt versions have a lot more face validity than do the biodata or covert forms. This should not be taken as an endorsement of overt tests, however, because face validity has almost nothing to do with whether or not a test can do what it claims. It just means that a test looks relevant.

Validity coefficients use the same scale (.00 to 1.00) as reliability coefficients, but deciding "how high is high enough?" is a lot more difficult and would require at least a chapter to explain. As a rule of thumb, though, it is rare to see a predictive (i.e., criterion-related) validity coefficient— the most critical type for an integrity test—above .60, and coefficients in the .30 to .40 range are commonly considered high (Kaplan & Saccuzzo, 1982).

REFERENCES

Allport, G.W. and Odbert, H.S. 1936. Trait names: a psycholexical study. *Psychological Monographs* 47, No. 211.

Ash, P. 1971. Screening employment applicants for attitudes toward theft. *Journal of Applied Psychology* 55: 161-64.

Bales, J. 1988. Integrity tests: Honest results? *The American Psychological Association Monitor* Aug., 1.

Caprino, M. 1989. Use of honesty tests growing. *The Marietta Daily Journal* 5 May, 3B.

Ganguli, H.C. 1985. Review of the Stanton Survey and the Stanton Survey Phase II. In *The ninth mental measurements yearbook*, J.C. Conoley and J.J. Kramer (Eds.). Lincoln, Nebraska: The University of Nebraska Press.

Gavzer, B. 1990. Should you tell all? *Parade* 27 May, 4-7.

Harte, S. 1990. Psychological testing: Debate rages over this worker screening tool. *The Atlanta Journal/Constitution* 2 April, 1.

Hartshorne, H., and May, M.A. 1928. *Studies in deceit.* New York: MacMillan.

Horne, J.L. 1972. Review of the Porteus Maze Test. In *The seventh mental measurements yearbook*, O.K. Buros (Ed.).

Jones, J.W. and Terris, W. 1983. Predicting employee's theft in home improvement centers. *Psychological Reports* 52, 187-201.

Kaplan, R., and Saccuzzo, D. 1982. *Psychological testing: Principles, applications, and issues.* Monterey, California: Brooks/Cole.

Kleinmuntz, B. 1989. Review of the Phase II Profile Integrity Status Inventory and ADdendum in *The tenth mental measurements yearbook*, J.C. Conoley and J.J. Kramer (Eds.). Lincoln, Nebraska: The University of Nebraska Press.

Lykken, D.T. 1981. *A tremor in the blood: Uses and abuses of the lie detector.* New York: McGraw-Hill.

Penner, L.A. 1986. *Social psychology: Concepts and applications*. St. Paul, Minnesota: West Publishing Co.

Rosenbaum, Richard W. 1976. Predictability of employee theft using weighted application blanks. *Journal of Applied Psychology* 61: 94-98.

Sackett, P., and Harris, M. 1984. Honesty testing for personnel selection: A review and critique. *Personnel Psychology* 37, 221-245.

Saxe, L. 1991. Lying: thoughts of an applied social psychologist. *American Psychologist* 46, 409-415.

Science Research Associates, Inc. 1987. *Personal Outlook Inventory examiner's manual.*

U.S. Congress, Office of Technology Assessment. 1990. The use of integrity tests for pre-employment screening. OTA-SET-442. Washington, D.C.: U.S. Government Printing Office.

Wheeler, K.G. 1985. Review of the Stanton Survey and the Stanton Survey Phase II. In *The ninth mental measurements yearbook*, J.C. Conoley and J.J. Kramer (Eds.). Lincoln, Nebraska: The University of Nebraska Press.